Entrepreneur
MAGAZINE'S

Kick-

Copywriting in
10 Easy Steps

Build the ***BUZZ*** *and*
Sell the *Sizzle*

Susan Gunelius ⊚ ⊚ ⊚

Jere L. Calmes, Publisher
Cover Design: Beth Hansen-Winter
Composition and Production: Lesley Rock for SquareOne Publishing Partners

This publication is designed to provide accurate and authoritative information
in regard to the subject matter covered. It is sold with the understanding that the
publisher is not engaged in rendering legal, accounting or other professional services.
If legal advice or other expert assistance is required, the services of a
competent professional person should be sought.

Library of Congress Cataloging-in-Publication Data

Gunelius, Susan M.
Kick-ass copywriting in 10 easy steps / by Susan M. Gunelius.
    p. cm.
ISBN-13: 978-1-59918-253-7 (alk. paper)
ISBN-10: 1-59918-253-X
1. Advertising copy—Handbooks, manuals, etc. I. Title.
HF5825.G86 2008
659.13'2—dc22

                                                                2008015791

Printed in Canada

11 10 09 08   10 9 8 7 6 5 4 3 2 1

DEDICATION

To Mom and Dad for your never-ending encouragement and support.

To Scott for picking up the slack while I wrote.

To Brynn, Daniel, and Ryan for the love and laughter you give.

Contents

Foreword

by Brian Clark

THERE ARE THREE QUICK AND VALUABLE POINTS I'D LIKE TO MAKE BEFORE you read this book.

1. The first point you might not believe at first.
2. The second point provides real-world proof that the first point is true.
3. And the third point is self evident thanks to the first two—you need to devour this book front to back, backward and forward, to take your business to the next level.

COPYWRITING IS A SUBJECT EVERY SMALL OR MEDIUM-SIZE BUSINESS OWNER MUST MASTER

I can already hear the objections.

How can *writing* be that important to business?

Don't worry . . . I know there's a lot involved with starting and running a business. I've started over half-a-dozen successful businesses in the last eight years (more about that in a minute).

But here's the thing . . .

Copywriting isn't about writing. Copywriting is about *selling*.

And sales are the most important thing to a small or medium-size business, right?

Effective selling is all about getting the right message to prospects and customers at the right time. And copywriting is all about crafting timely messages that sell.

Effective copywriting shifts your messages away from *what you want to say* toward *what people want to hear*, and it can be a magical thing. It can take your business from ordinary to legendary.

As a business owner, it's your job to create the optimal selling strategy for your products or services. It's not something you should outsource or delegate . . . it's up to you.

Those who understand the principles of copywriting know how to craft an effective selling strategy. Even if they never personally write a word of copy themselves.

That's why copywriting is a subject every small or medium-size business owner must master. And you're well on your way thanks to the book you're holding right now.

This brings us to point two.

COPYWRITING LANDED ME ON THIS BEACH IN MEXICO

I have a confession to make.

I'm a bit late getting this foreword done because I am goofing off with buddies down in Mexico. Copywriting combined with technology allows me to run my businesses from anywhere in the world, and I try to take advantage of that as much as possible (even in the middle of the week).

It wasn't always this way. Back in 1994, I graduated from law school sure of only one thing . . . I didn't want to be an attorney. It took me four years to break free from the law, determined to be an entrepreneur.

> Effective copywriting shifts your messages away from what you want to say toward what people want to hear.

And for the two years that followed, I floundered around. I had some limited success but nothing close to what I was hoping for.

Then I became a student of copywriting and everything changed.

Acting on what I learned, I quickly entered the highly competitive real estate brokerage field and within three months began generating a higher profit than most of my competitors. In 2005, I cashed out before the market went south.

The secret of my success?

I simply used effective sales copy to speak to prospective clients in the way they wanted to be spoken to. I delivered a message that was about them, not me.

And that made all the difference.

Nowadays, each new business I start is Internet-based and copy-driven, which allows me the freedom to goof off in Mexico in the middle of the week. Freedom (and enough money to enjoy it) is what success means to me.

This book can bring exceptional success to you, too.

THIS COPYWRITING BOOK IS THE KEY TO ACCELERATED BUSINESS SUCCESS

There are plenty of copywriting books around but none that so clearly addresses the real-life realities the business owner faces. Susan Gunelius understands copywriting, but more importantly, she understands business.

Susan lays out for you—in 10 easy and crystal-clear steps—the path to greater growth, profit, and wealth for people who conduct business in the real world. No theory or speculation, just time-tested tactics and strategies that work for small to middle-size business.

So don't hesitate . . . dive right in today. If you apply what you're about to discover to your business, I have no doubt that you'll be enjoying greater success and prosperity in no time.

See you on the beach.

Brian Clark
Copyblogger.com
April 23, 2008
Cabo San Lucas, Mexico

Preface

ITHINK MY LOVE OF COPYWRITING BEGAN WHEN I WAS IN HIGH SCHOOL. I always enjoyed writing, but it was when I was a teenager that I realized I enjoyed persuasive writing. I was probably the only 15-year-old in the world to have a large collection of print ads. I always believed that my mother thought I was crazy for collecting the ads because many of them were for alcohol. I'm sure she thought I had some kind of addictive personality. Ironically, years later, it turns out that's true. I'm addicted to chocolate and Diet Coke, but I digress. The point is that I loved print ads. From the design to the words, I loved everything about them, and I still do.

During my junior year of high school, my French teacher told me I had an uncanny ability to say a lot in very few words. To this day, I don't know if that was a compliment, but I took it as one. There's an old saying that everyone has some hidden talent, you just have to find out what it is. Well, mine was marketing and copywriting, and it kind of found me.

While I really wanted to study graphic design, I chose to pursue a degree in marketing—thinking it would make me more marketable once I graduated from college. From there, I started at the bottom working in a marketing support role for a division of AT&T. Luckily, the powers that be noticed that I had a knack for writing, and I was promoted to a position specifically created for me that allowed me to focus on marketing communications. That's where the pieces of my career started to fall into place. I realized that what I truly loved was the creative side of marketing, including copywriting, design, and production.

My interest and expertise grew over the next decade, which brings me to where I am today—writing about copywriting. In fact, my experience allows me to bring a unique perspective to authoring a book about copywriting. Rather than coming from the advertising agency side, my career was spent working on the client side. As I developed marketing programs and wrote copy, I did so by having the point of view of the business' goals and objectives in mind. I wasn't writing ads to put another notch on my creative belt or add another piece to my portfolio. Instead, I was writing copy to drive profits and add to the bottom line of the organization. The success of the marketing programs (and the accompanying copy) was in many ways a direct result of my efforts to define short and long-term objectives, track the results, and develop future marketing initiatives. I took beginning-to-end responsibility for marketing programs and advertising campaigns just like a small or medium-size business owner does when he or she invests in an ad or marketing program. My background gives me a slightly different perspective on marketing and advertising and a keen understanding of copywriting as a direct link to sales and profits. This is the perspective business owners and freelancers need to understand, too. Copywriting is more than just words. It's a brand, a promise, and a catalyst to sales.

I spent too many years watching local television ads and cringing as I witnessed small business owners waste money because of the horrendous copywriting used in their ads. My father owned a small business when I was growing up, so I completely understand the budgetary constraints that a small business owner faces. Money is simply not there to hire a professional copywriter.

With the goal of helping small and medium-size business owners, I sat down to write *Kick-ass Copywriting in 10 Easy Steps*. Not long after I started writing, I began communicating with other writers through several online forums. Repeatedly, I heard writers with no copywriting or marketing experience say they planned to transition to copywriting. These declarations concerned me because I feared more and more poorly written ads would surface and continue to work against the business owners who paid for and depended on them. Copywriting is very different from other forms of writing such as expository writing. There is much more that goes into writing compelling copy than people realize and successfully segueing into a copywriting career is not as easy as it sounds.

Along the way, this book turned into more than just a tool for small and medium-size business owners. My goal in writing this book is to help small and medium-size business owners as well as eBay sellers, Craigslist sellers, nonprofessional and beginner copywriters, freelancers, and anyone else who does not have a background in marketing and copywriting learn how to write effective, sales-oriented copy that increases sales and boosts profits.

Now for some final administrative notes: all real-world product and company names and copywriting samples are trademarks of their respective owners. Attempts were made to obtain permissions for the use of copyrighted material. I apologize for any instances in which copyrighted material was used inadvertently without obtaining permission. I will be happy to rectify the omission in future editions. Real-world ad examples in Chapter 15 were designed by Kulture Marketing (www.KultureMarketing.com).

I hope this book teaches you to write copy that meets your goals and builds your business. Now, let's stop talking and let's start copywriting!

Susan Gunelius
January 2008

Acknowledgments

KICK-ASS COPYWRITING IN 10 EASY STEPS **IS THE RESULT OF A LIFETIME OF** writing and marketing experience. With that said, there are many people who helped me get to the point in my life and career where writing this book became possible. I'll do my best to acknowledge those people here, but in many cases, words simply aren't enough to convey my gratitude.

First, I have to thank my parents, Bill and Carol Ann Henry, for their constant encouragement and support. From the time I was a young child, they encouraged my writing and their words of support did not fall on deaf ears. Copywriting has always come naturally to me, and I love it. Writing a book has always been one of my goals in life. *Kick-ass Copywriting in 10 Easy Steps* is my second book, so I've reached that goal and for that I thank my parents.

Where would I be without my husband, Scott? Probably still working in the corporate world enjoying my role in the marketing field but not pursuing my true dreams and goals. With my husband as my partner, I know I can accomplish anything

I set out to do. His support keeps me going and is a constant reminder that I can do it when I doubt myself.

Of course, my children, Brynn, Daniel, and Ryan, inspire me everyday. They don't even know it yet, but they also played a part in helping me write this book. Without them, I may not have pursued working from home and writing for myself.

To Leslie List from Kulture Marketing for helping me gather the ad samples used in Chapter 15, and to Lesley Rock at SquareOne Publishing Partners for patiently making this book look great.

To my agent, Bob Diforio, and to Jere Calmes at Entrepreneur Press, thank you for recognizing I have something to say and letting me say it.

Introduction

WHETHER YOU'RE A SMALL BUSINESS OWNER, A MEDIUM-SIZE BUSINESS owner, an eBay seller, or simply trying to break into the copywriting industry, *Kick-ass Copywriting in 10 Easy Steps* will help you understand the fundamentals of writing sales-oriented copy and put you on a path to success. At its core, copywriting is another device in a business' marketing toolbox. Well-written copy can make or break an ad or marketing piece. With that in mind, copywriting can equate to either well-spent advertising investments or a waste of advertising dollars.

Many people misinterpret the uniqueness of effective copywriting. I can't count the number of times I've heard freelance writers say they want to shift from article writing to copywriting as if it's simply an extension of their existing abilities. Copywriting does come naturally to some people, but for most, it's a foreign landscape they do not know how to navigate. Copywriting is about more than writing the hard-sell sales letter that many short copywriting courses offer. In fact, I cringe when I see those over-the-top sales letters, which do little more than provide an ugly representation of copywriting, sales, and marketing.

Well-crafted copywriting doesn't need to beat a person over the head. It doesn't have to drown in bold typeface and capitalization. The message should stand on its own without an overabundance of heavy-handed sales language and design embellishments. I associate many sales letters that are guilty of this technique with a writer who doesn't truly understand the basic purpose of copywriting. *Kick-ass Copywriting in 10 Easy Steps* will teach you how to write effective copy, so you will not only boost sales but also look like a seasoned professional.

THERE'S MORE TO COPYWRITING THAN JUST WRITING

Copywriting is not as much about what you say as how you say it. The goal of copywriting is to communicate to your existing or potential customers and convince them to buy your product, ask for additional information, or contact you. Before you sit down to write copy, you need to define the end goal for the ad, marketing piece, or business communication you're creating and then align your copywriting to meet these goals. I think most noncopy-writers don't understand how much goes on behind the scenes before writing copy. The writing process is actually just a small fraction of the steps necessary to produce effective copywriting. Copy is the outcome of a clear understanding of the benefits of your product, its differentiators from your competition, the emotional triggers of your customers, and more. In fact, it's the research, organization, and thought process that happen before your pen touches the paper that truly dictates your copywriting success.

Let me share a story that demonstrates my point. Not long ago, I saw a commercial on television for a local car dealership featuring the business owner and his pet parrot. The script was tailored to the limited vocabulary skills of the bird who did most of the talking in the commercial. The copy neither communicated the features, benefits, or differentiators of the dealership nor did it appeal to the audience's emotional triggers. In fact, it seemed more like a home movie than a commercial intended to boost sales. Unfortunately, the owner's feathered friend could not communicate an effective message beyond simply telling viewers to visit the dealership. The likelihood of anyone being compelled to buy a car from this dealership based on this poorly worded script recited by a parrot is slim to none. Of course, there are bird lovers who may have been intrigued by the commercial, but this group of people represents just a small fraction of car buyers.

While the concept of including the parrot in the commercial was not the best choice, there were ways to make the concept work with well-written copy. After all, it's copy that sells products and services far more frequently than the concept of the ad. If the owner of the car dealership knew how to create sales-oriented copy, he may not have wasted his advertising dollars with an ad that did little more than showcase his pet.

This leads me to another point. Copywriting is an essential component of advertising and marketing success. A great ad concept or graphic design should simply enhance the message communicated by your copy. Great copy should stand on its own without any reliance on a design. Most graphic designers will disagree with this statement, but I stand by it. I love graphic design, but I do believe that in advertising the message is more important than the design. Ultimately, the two should work together to make the strongest ad or marketing piece possible. That's why it's important to understand design as you write copy. Take the time to speak with your designer or do some research on your own to educate yourself on the basic elements of design. This knowledge will help you construct a marketing piece that effectively communicates your message while being visually appealing to your audience. Together, these two components are exceptionally powerful.

STRAIGHT FROM THE REAL WORLD

Nothing can help explain the elements of effective copywriting better than real-world examples. Each chapter of this book focuses on a step in the Copywriting Outline (Chapter 2) and is interspersed with fictitious small business copywriting examples as well as real-world, well-known examples. From Brylcreem to Burger King, you'll see how effective copywriting helped boost profits for some of the largest companies in the world. In addition, Chapters 15 and 16 provide a collection of real-world and practical copywriting examples from small and medium-size businesses to further demonstrate the techniques and theories discussed in this book. *Kick-ass Copywriting in 10 Easy Steps* will show you how to use tried and true copywriting methods to create your own sales-driven advertising and marketing campaigns. So get your pen, and let's get started!

chapter one

Don't Be Intimidated by Copywriting— Be Inspired!

COPYWRITING CAN BE SIMPLE

You can write effective sales-generating advertising, marketing, and business communications copy. In fact, you can start right now by understanding the first tenet of copywriting:

> Your product or service is far less important than its ability to fulfill your customers' needs.

I'll explain why this principle is so important throughout this book. For now, take a few minutes to write the first tenet of copywriting down. Post it by your computer, telephone, cash register, bedside table, or anywhere it will act as a constant reminder. The first tenet of copywriting should permeate into *all* your business activities. Why is the first tenet of copywriting so important? It's simple. At the end of the day, it doesn't matter how wonderful your product is if it doesn't benefit customers by helping them in some way. This concept will be discussed in

Your product or service is far less important than its ability to fulfill your customers' needs.

great detail throughout this book, but here in the first chapter, it's sufficient for you to understand that *Kick-ass Copywriting in 10 Easy Steps* is exactly what its name implies. It will teach you how to write compelling copy one simple step at a time. Imagine this book as a successful copywriter's hand holding yours as you take each step necessary to write copy that sells. Don't be intimidated by copywriting—be inspired!

COPYWRITING IS NOT JUST SMOKE AND MIRRORS

What is copywriting? It's the use of words to drive an audience (typically consumers) to action. More importantly, copywriting is one element of your marketing toolkit. In order to build awareness and recognition of your product or service and ultimately drive sales, you can use a variety of marketing tools including placing ads (that is, buying ad space or time in television, radio, internet, or a print publication), handing out brochures, sending direct mail or email, creating a website, and much more. To ensure that these tools produce the results you want, you need to communicate with appropriate and compelling words. These words create the message your ad or marketing tool conveys to consumers and are called "copy." Crafting these words is copywriting, but a great deal of research, thought, and analysis needs to be done to write effective copy. This book will show you how to easily work through these steps.

Advertising agencies make novice copywriters think only experts can effectively execute the craft. Based on what ad agency account managers tell

CLOSEUP

The First Tenet of Copywriting
Your product or service is far less important than its ability to fulfill your customers' needs.

their potential clients, you would think only Shakespeare could create copy that sells products. (Isn't it lucky that the agency just happens to have Shakespearean copywriters on staff who have the special talents and experience necessary to rise to the challenge?) Remember, it's copy, not *Macbeth*. When people are considering buying a product, they are not thinking in Shakespearean terms but rather in quite simple terms. Sure they'll weigh options and compare features and prices (particularly with larger purchases), but the final purchase decision is a very basic one.

Similarly, copywriting is quite simple when you look at its basic purpose. You have a product to sell. Who wants your product and why? How can you compel these people to act and buy your product? Copy that sells products appeals to consumers' needs. Remember the first tenet of copywriting, "Your product or service is far less important than its ability to fulfill your customers' needs." It's essential to understand that consumers may not even realize that they have a need. Great copy makes people not only think they want your product; it makes people think they *need* your product.

> Copywriting is more than words. It's a promise, a brand, and a catalyst to sales.

In official marketing terminology, this process is called creating a "perceived need." Advertising and marketing is all about creating perceived needs, but remember, this book is going to illustrate you how simple copywriting can be; it will show you that you can write copy that sells even if you're just starting out in the copywriting business or have no formal training. Instead of using industry terms and buzzwords like "perceived need," let's call copywriting what it is at its most basic level—seducing someone to act in a certain way through the use of persuasive language.

That's right. The best copywriters can convince consumers to buy things they don't need. Do people need a Mercedes? No. Do people need an automatic dishwasher? No. The copywriter's job is to persuade consumers into thinking they need these items when, in fact, they are not essential. They might look good or make life a bit easier, but no one truly needs these items. However, companies are selling nonessentials at a staggering rate. How do they do it? The answer is simple. They do it with great advertising copy that convinces consumers to give up their hard-earned money in exchange for a product or service.

INEFFECTIVE COPYWRITING = WASTED MONEY AND LOST OPPORTUNITY

Television, radio, newspapers, and other print publications are wrought with examples of wasted local advertising dollars due to poor copywriting. Too often, small business owners rely on the inexperienced, inadequately trained copywriter provided by the medium in which they are placing their advertisement. Many ads in the business section of the local telephone book or local newspaper are perfect examples of this practice of offering copywriting services for a fee. Many small business owners accept this service, and their ads reflect an evident lack of professional copywriting.

Local television commercials provide slightly different but equally effective examples of poor copywriting that fails to drive sales, or in some cases, even succeeds at driving customers to the competition. I recently saw a television commercial for a local mattress store that proves my point tenfold. The copy for the script contained little more than, "Making commercials isn't easy but buying a mattress is at The Mattress Store." The owner read the copy and was supported by an animated character depicting the owner in various blooper scenes simulating mistakes made during the filming of the commercial. Not only does the copy fail to drive sales to The Mattress Store, but it also succeeds at driving customers *away* from The Mattress Store.

As a potential customer, I found nothing compelling about the commercial. It included no benefits for me and provided no differentiators from other mattress stores. It failed to follow the first tenet of copywriting, *"Your product or service is far less important than its ability to fulfill your customers' needs."* All I came away with was a negative impression of the owner. (He had such a big ego that he made himself into a cartoon character!) In fact, this probably would be one of the last stores I would visit to buy a mattress. After all, I was given no compelling reason to think differently. Bottom line, the concept for the commercial was terrible, and the copy, which could have saved the poor concept, failed to deliver in any of the most basic principles of writing sales-driven copy.

I'm not saying there aren't times when a good concept can't make a commercial very successful, but you should not rely on a concept to drive sales. The success of a concept-driven ad that is not supported by effective copywriting is typically short lived. On the other hand, concept-driven commercials that also use compelling copywriting can be significantly successful. Consider the Wendy's "Where's the beef?" commercial from the 1980s. The concept was extremely popular, but ultimately, it simply supported the copy that differentiated Wendy's large hamburgers from the smaller hamburgers offered by fast food competitors.

Similarly, in this decade, we see the success of the GEICO commercials featuring cavemen characters. The concept was so popular that it even was used to launch a short-lived television sitcom. While the concept of the commercials is appealing to a wide audience, it actually enhances the true message of the copy: switching to GEICO insurance is "So easy, even a caveman can do it." I'll discuss the relationship between ad concepts or design with copywriting in further detail in Chapter 14. For now, it's important to understand that copywriting drives the success of ads more often than concepts or designs, but together, copy, concept, and design can create a cohesive, powerful marketing campaign.

BEFORE YOU BEGIN, SET YOUR GOALS

Before you begin writing copy for any ad or marketing piece, you need to know why you're writing it. You must set time-sensitive goals for your marketing tactics before you move forward on executing them, and these goals should be quantifiable to be useful in helping you develop marketing strategies in the future. By setting goals, you will be able to track the results of your marketing materials against your objectives to determine their success and calculate your return on investment (ROI). This analysis will help you determine where to invest your advertising budget going forward, so you only invest money in the ads and marketing pieces that deliver the biggest bang for the buck. Some examples of time-sensitive, quantifiable goals you might set for your advertising or marketing investments include the following (note that numbers and dates in these examples are fictitious and are for demonstration purposes only):

- Generate 100 new customers by December 31st.
- Generate 500 customer leads in the form of mailing addresses by December 31st for future promotional mailings.
- Generate 200 repeat customers by December 31st.
- Reduce inventory of Super Sharp Lawn Mowers by 400 units by December 31st.
- Reduce customer service calls by 20% by December 31st.
- Generate awareness of new delivery service by receiving 150 inquiries by December 31st.
- Increase the number of customers requesting delivery and installation services by 20% by December 31st.
- Increase holiday season store traffic by 25% between November 26th and December 24th.
- Increase customer referrals by 30% by December 31st.

DON'T JUST DEFINE YOUR PRODUCT—SHOWCASE IT

The purpose of copywriting is not to provide a dictionary definition or encyclopedic knowledge of your product. Instead, copywriting is meant to showcase your product. Think of copywriting as a parade where each element of copy represents a float. Each element of copy is meant to speak directly to the audience, appeal to that audience, and mean something to that audience. During a parade, there inevitably will be a float or exhibit that simply doesn't hold the attention of viewers. The same can happen with copywriting; one element could be meaningless to the audience. Unlike the parade, where the audience will stick around to see the next float, your audience will not stick around long enough to see if the next sentence in your ad is better. Your job as a copywriter is to make sure that every word and phrase you use in a marketing piece helps to move your customers to action and allows you to meet the goals and return on investment requirements defined for the marketing effort. Effective copywriting gets to the point and doesn't deviate, ensuring that your audience will not walk away.

REMEMBER WHAT YOU WANT YOUR COPY TO DO

Before you start any copywriting project, it's important to identify what you want your copy to do. More often than not, you will write copy to persuade your customers to act in some way such as make a purchase, visit your store or website, call you, make an inquiry, schedule an appointment, place an order, or some other activity that generates sales and profits for your

☼ CLOSEUP

The Four Actions of Effective Copy

1. **Drive** your customers to act through your copy
2. **Motivate** your customers to act through your copy
3. **Compel** your customers to act through your copy
4. **Persuade** your customers to act through your copy

Keep the Four Actions of Effective Copywriting in mind as you write copy, so you keep focused on the ultimate goal of writing action-oriented copy.

business. Don't simply suggest an action in your copy—demand it. (See Closeup Box for the Four Actions of Effective Copy.)

THE ROLE OF COPYWRITING IN SUCCESSFUL ADVERTISING AND MARKETING

Each ad or marketing piece you create is developed with a purpose or final goal in mind. Whether the purpose is to generate awareness of a new product or increase repeat purchases, advertising strategies follow the same basic

 **CLOSEUP**

The Seven Steps of Advertising Success

1. **Awareness:** Consumers move from an unaware state to being aware of a product or brand.

2. **Recognition:** Consumers remember and associate a product or brand to a previous experience (for example, an advertisement or promotion).

3. **Interest:** Consumers become curious about a product or brand leading them to ask questions or research it to learn more about it.

4. **Purchase:** Consumers understand the product or brand enough to motivate them to buy it.

5. **Repurchase:** Consumers are satisfied with the product or brand after their first purchase and are motivated to buy it again.

6. **Loyalty:** Consumers are so satisfied with the product or brand that they buy it again and again choosing it over other products or brands and potentially traveling to different locations to find it.

7. **Influencer:** Loyal consumers are so satisfied with the product or brand that they are motivated to talk about it with others and promote the product through word-of-mouth marketing.

steps. I call these steps the Seven Steps of Advertising Success (see Closeup Box).

Before you write copy for an advertisement or marketing piece, it's important to define the goals for that piece and determine where that piece fits in the Seven Steps of Advertising Success. If your goal is to generate new customers, then messages such as, "The taste you love," won't motivate your target audience because they have no prior experience with your product and no idea if they love the taste of it or not. A better copy message to an audience of prospective customers might say, "You'll love the refreshing taste." Alternatively, if your goal is to generate repeat customers then a message like, "The taste you love," is very appropriate because that target audience is already familiar with your product.

Every word in your copy should be there for a specific reason.

Ultimately, you want to effectively place ads and marketing materials that communicate a compelling message to move your customers through the Seven Steps of Advertising Success. By following these seven steps in your marketing and advertising plans, you'll be able to create copy that speaks to your customers at each stage of their experience with your product. The goal is to obtain new customers, motivate them to try your product again, make them emotionally attached and loyal to it, and finally, have them talk about it, boosting word-of-mouth marketing and drawing in new customers. It's a linear and cyclical path, and it's every marketer's ideal objective.

GET STARTED NOW WITH AN OUTLINE FOR SUCCESS

Copywriting seems intimidating for nonprofessionals not only because they think they don't have the creative flair required to write successfully, but also because they don't know what information is essential to drive their customers to action. Alternatively, they don't understand the importance of copywriting. Frequently, I hear freelance writers and business owners downplay the importance of copywriting—claiming it's easy and anyone can do it. That's true. Anyone can sing, too, but that doesn't mean everyone *should* sing. Writing is one of those activities that everyone is capable of doing, but there are many types of writing with different requirements for achieving success. To be a good writer, you need to understand the nuances of each genre, style, medium, and more. For example, just because someone can write a nonfiction book doesn't mean they can write poetry; they are two very different types of writing. Similarly, just because a person can write a fiction book doesn't mean they can write a speech or ad copy or a newsletter.

Each type of writing is very different from the next and each requires different knowledge to execute it well. This knowledge separates good copy from poorly written, amateur copy and separates ads that sell from ads that don't sell. Each ad or marketing piece you produce has associated costs such as printing, placement, and so on. Poorly written copy can negate any other efforts related to that marketing initiative. No matter how much money you spend on the perfect placement for your ad (perhaps on the back cover of the best magazine), if your copy isn't first-rate, your ad will not produce optimum results, and you won't get the return on your investment that you need and deserve.

Learning to write sales-oriented copy begins with giving up either the idea that you're not creative, and therefore aren't capable of copywriting, or the idea that anyone can write copy. The first step in leaving these precon- ceived notions behind is to learn what goes on behind the scenes before you actually write any copy. First, you need to get organized, and the best way to do that is to get the most important information about you, your company, and your product or service down on paper. I call this the Copywriting Outline.

chapter two

Get Organized with the Copywriting Outline

WHAT IS A COPYWRITING OUTLINE?

The purpose of the Copywriting Outline (see Figure 2.1 for a snapshot of the Copywriting Outline) is to put all your thoughts about your product in one place. I created the Copywriting Outline to help small and medium-size business owners and beginner copywriters complete the necessary background work before copywriting can begin in a methodical, linear way. The Copywriting Outline provides a single tool where you record all the details about your product or service that you will need to produce compelling copy again and again. It's also an evolving instrument that you add to as your product or business changes and grows.

Your Copywriting Outline acts as a single source of information about your product or service, and each step in the Copywriting Outline represents an area you need to research and fully understand before you can begin crafting marketing messages. Remember, copywriting is about creating perceived needs among a specific audience. For example, how can you attempt to create perceived needs if you don't first understand the benefits of your product, who your audience is, and where you will communicate with them? The steps you complete before you begin writing copy are crucial to the ultimate success of your marketing campaign. If you skip these beginning steps, your advertising message will lose some of its power when you write your copy.

If you have a broad product line or diverse clientele, you might want to create a separate Copywriting Outline for each product or customer group. The reason for this is simple. Each product in your product line provides different benefits and differentiators and each customer group (called "marketing segments" in official marketing terminology) within your current and prospective end-user audience has different needs and desires. Don't fall into the trap of trying to take short cuts with your copywriting research. If there are fundamental differences between your products and the audiences for them,

CLOSEUP

The Ten Steps to Copywriting Success

1. Exploit your product's benefits
2. Exploit your competition's weaknesses
3. Know your audience
4. Communicate W.I.I.F.M. (What's In It For Me)
5. Focus on "you," not "we"
6. Know your medium
7. Avoid too much information
8. Include a call to action
9. C.Y.A. (Cover Your Ass)
10. Proofread

take the time up-front to develop a comprehensive Copywriting Outline for each product and each audience. The work you do now will pay off tenfold in the future by saving you time and money when you sit down to write the most compelling copy possible that drives results and boosts profits.

DOING THE WORK NOW SAVES TIME AND MONEY LATER

Each time you want to create an advertising or promotional campaign you can refer to your Copywriting Outline to cull the best attributes and benefits related to your product for that particular program. Then, simply organize the points from your Copywriting Outline, add in some action words, and the first draft of the copy for your ad is done. It truly can be that simple, and this book will show you the principles you'll need to follow to extract the copy points from your Copywriting Outline and put them together into compelling sales copy. If you take the time up-front to create a detailed Copywriting Outline, you'll reap the rewards in the long term.

While reading this book, begin the copywriting process by filling in the information for your product, service, or business in the Copywriting Outline template in Appendix A. The Copywriting Outline follows the order of the chapters in this book. As you read and learn about copywriting principles and how to develop compelling copywriting through tips and useful examples, take notes in your own Copywriting Outline with information about your products and business. In the future, when you update your outline with changes to your products, audience, or advertising opportunities, you can refer back to the corresponding chapters in this book if you need help developing certain sections. Remember, the Copywriting Outline is a working document. It's never complete, and it's always changing. If you don't update it, the outline will lose its usefulness.

The Copywriting Outline is a working document. As long as your business changes and grows, it will never be complete.

Not only is the Copywriting Outline helpful in producing sales messages, but it also can be useful in other areas of your business. If you take the time to maintain a current and comprehensive Copywriting Outline, you will have a tool that provides a cogent overview of your product line and marketing plan. Think of the many ways your Copywriting Outline could be adapted to other parts of your business including securing capital investments, attracting business partners, and much more. With simple modifications, your Copywriting Outline can transform into a very useful tool to help support and grow your business.

As you write, use the basic elements of copy as jumping off points to help you create complete messages.

It may take some time to get organized, but once you complete your Copywriting Outline, creating sales-driven copy won't seem quite so intimidating. You've already done 90% of the work. Writing the copy is the easy part once you have your goals and information captured in your Copywriting Outline.

THE ELEMENTS OF COPY

Before you read the remainder of this book and begin completing your Copywriting Outline, it's important to understand the elements of copy. Copywriting is more than just writing words. There are different pieces that go into creating the copy for each advertisement or marketing piece. While every element is not always used in every ad or marketing piece, the following is an overview of some of the most important elements of copywriting:

- **Headline:** The headline is intended to grab your audience's attention and convince them to look at your ad further. The key to writing an effective headline is to get to the point.

FIGURE 2.1
Copywriting Outline

Step 1: Exploit Your Product's Benefits—How is my product better than other, similar products available (i.e., the competition)? Why is my product the best?

Step 2: Exploit Your Competition's Weaknesses—How are my competitors' products inferior to mine?

Step 3: Know Your Audience—Who should buy my product or who is likely to want or need it (i.e., target audience/market)? Who will see my ad?

Step 4: Communicate W.I.I.F.M. (What's In It For Me?)—How can I elaborate on my product's benefits and differentiators to tell customers specifically how my product will affect their lives in a positive manner?

Step 5: Focus on "You," Not "We"—How can I word my product's benefits and differentiators, so they talk *to* the customer and not *about* me?

Step 6: Know Your Medium—Where will I be advertising? How can I write copy to maximize the space provided by that medium?

Step 7: Avoid T.M.I. (Too Much Information)—What information is important to me but not helpful in an ad (i.e., may be useful in a news article or brochure in the future)? How can I keep my ad copy from becoming cluttered?

Step 8: Include a Call to Action—What do I want my customers to do as soon as they read my ad? How can I create a sense of urgency?

Step 9: C.Y.A. (Cover Your Ass)—What are some phrases I want to remember to include in my ads to protect myself? Is there anything else I need to remember to back up my claims?

Step 10: Proofread—Who can proofread my ad for me? What tools are available to help me proofread my ad?

- **Subhead:** The subhead expounds on the headline. While the headline is meant to catch your audience's attention, the subhead gives them a bit more information and works with the headline to tease your audience to read more or listen further.

- **Key selling points:** The key selling points are the elements of your copy that communicate the primary benefits or differentiators of your product or service. This is where you provide details that persuade customers to believe they need your product or service.

- **Special offer:** A special offer is included if your ad or marketing piece is intended to communicate a sale, discount, or other promotion.

- **Call to action with contact information:** The call to action is used to invoke a sense of urgency to the ad and give the audience clear directions on how to respond to the ad. This is where you tell the audience what you want them to do.

- **Tracking mechanism:** You might want to include a method to track the results of your ad through a special code, website address, or phone number to determine if the ad meets your return on investment objectives.

- **Additional information:** Sometimes you'll need to provide additional information about your product or service to further clarify your message. This is common with highly complex product advertisements such as technical or medical equipment. Depending on the product or service being advertised, you'll need to determine the importance of the additional information to decide what priority to give it in your copy.

- **Disclaimers:** You need to include disclaimers to protect yourself and your business against potential lawsuits or negative publicity.

Regardless of the type of marketing piece you're writing, your copy should focus on these elements. Whether you're creating a radio ad or an in-depth brochure, your marketing copy should be structured similarly in terms of catching the attention of your audience, teasing them to look or listen further, providing your key selling points, describing your offers, and telling them how to respond. Take some time to analyze ads in magazines or brochures that were most likely written by professional copywriters and try to find the copywriting elements used in each piece. You'll undoubtedly find a pattern showing that the same elements are typically used to communicate marketing messages through effective copywriting.

chapter three

step one
Exploit Your Product's Benefits

FEATURES VS. BENEFITS

The first step of the Copywriting Outline is the foundation for your advertising campaigns. A benefit is the value of your product to a customer. In other words, a benefit is what the product can do for a customer or how the product can help a customer. You need to put into words the reasons your product is the best available and better than your competitors' products based on the added value it provides to your customers. The key to success is for you to fully understand all the benefits of your product. Only then can you ensure that the audience knows them and can relate to them.

Most people confuse a product feature with a product benefit. During my undergraduate studies, my Introduction to Marketing professor spent countless classroom hours drilling students in identifying features vs. benefits. In simple terms, features are like features on your face. For example, the features on your face include two eyes, a nose, and a

LEARNING OBJECTIVES

The difference between benefits and features

How to communicate benefits

How descriptive words can enhance your copy

Emotional triggers and how to appeal to them in your copy

mouth. What are the benefits of those features? Since I'm hungry right now, the first benefits that come to mind include:

- Your eyes allow you to see the colors, shapes, and textures of a fabulously presented meal.
- Your nose lets you smell the delicious food.
- Your mouth allows you to taste the delicious food.

Of course, since your eyes, nose, and mouth are windows to your senses, the benefits I first thought of are related to those senses. The features on your face allow you to do something you want to do, or they do it for you. The same can be said of any product. The features of your product will help your customer in some way. The benefits are *how* the product will help the customer.

Another way to help understand the difference between features and benefits is to substitute the following words for benefits:

- Betterment
- Gain
- Godsend
- Perk

Sometimes it's easier to call benefits betterments or perks to clearly see the difference between features and benefits. Instead of asking yourself what benefits your product delivers to customers, ask yourself what perks or betterments your product delivers or what your customers stand to gain if they use your product. Alternatively, think of what it is about your product that would make a customer say, "This product is a godsend."

Understanding the difference between features and benefits is a common stumbling block even for professional marketers and copywriters. It takes years of experience to get very good at quickly translating features into benefits, but with a bit of time and effort, nonprofessional and beginner copywriters can develop a list of their product's benefits. In fact, the easiest way to start creating benefits is to first make a list of all your product's features. Then, next to each feature describe how it will benefit or help a user. (See the Closeup Box for examples of the difference between features and benefits.)

Next, personalize each benefit and explicitly tell your audience what it can do for them. (I'll explain this in more detail in Step 4 of the Copywriting Outline, W.I.I.F.M. (What's In It For Me?) Once you're able to connect your

 **CLOSEUP**

Features vs. Benefits for Suck-Up Vacuum Cleaner

Below is a list of features and a corresponding benefit for each feature to help demonstrate the difference between features and benefits and how describing benefits, rather than simply listing features, can be used effectively in copywriting to create a perceived need among consumers.

- **Feature:** Lightweight (10 lbs.)
  - **Benefit:** You won't strain your back carrying Suck-up Vacuum up and down the stairs.
- **Feature:** On board tools
  - **Benefit:** Save time. No more searching for the furniture brush. It's stored in the convenient compartment on the back of Suck-up Vacuum.
- **Feature:** Bagless
  - **Benefit:** Save money. No more bags to buy.
- **Feature:** 5-year warranty
  - **Benefit:** Peace of mind. No worries if your Suck-up Vacuum stops working.
- **Feature:** HEPA filter
  - **Benefit:** Better for your health. Suck-up Vacuum will leave your house cleaner than ever before. Even the smallest speck of dust and debris is removed when you use Suck-up Vacuum leaving your house cleaner than ever before.

product's benefits directly to your audience, you'll be on the road to increased sales.

Do your market research! Ask your current customers why they buy your product or service. What features do they like, and how do those features benefit them?

THINK LIKE THE CUSTOMER

Now that you can identify the difference between features and benefits, you can complete the first step of your Copywriting Outline. List all the features of your product or service (you can modify the list as your product changes in the future). Even the smallest feature, which seems insignificant to you, could turn into an actionable benefit for your customers. Once you have your features listed, take some time to imagine you're the customer. What would you look for in this product? What would you want the product to help you do or do for you? Sometimes working backward like this can make writing benefits easier.

BE AN INVESTIGATIVE JOURNALIST

While copywriting is very different from journalism, the research behind the process is very similar. Before you begin writing copy, you need to understand your goals and the benefits of your product in order to create a compelling, actionable message. For example, when you're working on the benefits section of your Copywriting Outline, don't just use your own opinion to identify the five best features and benefits of your product. Those features and benefits might not be the most important ones to your customers depending on where, when, and what you're advertising. To ensure the benefits section of your Copywriting Outline is comprehensive, take some time to research key journalistic questions, including:

1. **Who:** Who will your product help? Break your customer list into segments of customers with unique characteristics (segmentation will be

discussed further in Chapter 4). Before you write your copy, you need to define who you want to see that copy.

2. **What:** What will your product do for your customers? Each customer segment is likely to want to gain different things from your products, and therefore, each segment will respond to different benefits language in your copy.

3. **Where:** Where will your product help customers? Most products have some element of location inherent to the product's use. For example, a high-speed blender might help customers spend less time in the kitchen and more time with loved ones. Alternatively, a cell phone may help consumers who drive long distances feel safe in their cars late at night.

4. **When:** Benefits copy can be written to appeal to a time factor. For example, a cell phone might provide peace of mind to parents by allowing them to stay continually connected to their teenage children.

5. **Why:** Perhaps the most important part of your journalistic research is to define why your message matters to consumers. Why should they care about you or your product? Make them care in your copy.

6. **How:** Ensure your audience understands how each item in your copywriting outline will directly affect their lives.

USING DESCRIPTIVE AND INFLUENTIAL WORDS

This is a good time to start thinking about the specific words you will use in your copywriting. Create a list of adjectives to describe the features and corresponding benefits of your product. Using compelling, descriptive language can immensely boost the effectiveness of your copy. For example, a restaurant owner could say, "We have delicious food," in his ad. However, if he included more effective descriptive words in his copy such as, "Let yourself indulge in our mouthwatering entrees and decadent desserts," the copy has a stronger impact. As a consumer, would you be more apt to visit the restaurant using the copy in the first or second example? I know I would choose the second example. It makes me curious to learn more, and it makes me hungry just reading the copy.

Another good example centers on a local cleaning service. Instead of copy that says, "We'll clean your home," compelling, descriptive copy could say, "Say goodbye to your smallest speck of dirt because we'll get your home white-glove clean." By using descriptive words like "smallest speck" and "white-glove," it is clear that this cleaning service goes above and beyond the typical cleaning service. When you are writing copy, you want to make your product or service stand out and have meaning to your customers by directly communicating with them on a personal level. Take some time to consult a thesaurus or look at other ads to see what words work well. Then create your own list of words and phrases that will help sell your product.

> Use powerful words, but don't go overboard. Your copy can quickly turn from compelling to unbelievable with too many "hard-sell" words.

One of the keys to writing descriptive copy is to appeal to the five senses of smell, taste, touch, sight, and sound. Great copy creates a complete sensory experience for the audience. As you write copy, use descriptive words and phrases to appeal to the five senses and make your audience feel like they are experiencing your product or service firsthand. In other words, create their experiences for them.

It's important to note that using descriptive words allows your copy to have a stronger impact, but these words can also make your copy sound unbelievable if they are overused or too far-fetched. Think of using descriptive words in the same way you use them in conversation. Imagine you see a friend driving a new Honda Civic. While certainly a nice car, it's unlikely you would tell your friend, "That is the most amazing car I've ever seen." The word *amazing* used to describe a Honda Civic doesn't seem believable. However, if your friend was driving a Lamborghini, perhaps *amazing* is appropriate. The same idea holds true in copywriting. Many

CLOSEUP

Descriptive Words and Phrases to Use with Caution in Copy
- Amazing
- Remarkable
- Outstanding
- Incredible
- Extraordinary
- Special
- Exclusive
- Can't live without
- One of a kind
- Just for you
- New
- No hassle
- No risk

descriptive words have lost their impact simply because they come across as false promises or pie-in-the-sky claims. Bottom line, use descriptive words but don't sacrifice the integrity of your copy for them.

APPEAL TO CUSTOMERS' EMOTIONAL TRIGGERS

As you identify your product's features and benefits, you should also determine how these features and benefits relate to consumers' emotions. Consumers are often motivated to buy by numerous emotional triggers. Think about your own emotional triggers when you make buying decisions, then create a list of emotional triggers that could affect customers who buy your product. Your copywriting should always appeal to these emotional triggers. Of course, some products and brands are more dependent on emotional triggers than others, which I will discuss in further detail in Chapter 14. Some examples of emotional triggers that you can leverage in your copywriting include:

- **Fear:** The emotion of fear in terms of consumer behavior can include the fear of being left behind or not fitting in with peers. (Example: "Don't get left behind.")
- **Competition:** The emotion of competition demonstrates the old adage of keeping up with the Joneses. (Example: "Be the envy of your neighborhood.")
- **Desire to be a leader:** This emotion is displayed by consumers known as "early adopters" in marketing terminology; people who like to be the first to try products and tell their friends and family about their latest finds. (Example: "Everyone in your neighborhood will want to try your new gas grill.")
- **Desire to be trendy or cool:** The emotional desire to be cool does not always go away after high school. Most people continue to want to stay current with trends long into adulthood. (Example: "Now you too can get the hottest new car in Hollywood.")
- **Need for instant gratification:** In today's society, everything has a sense of urgency, from waiting in line at the grocery store to commuting to work to making a purchase. (Example: "Drive home today in your new car.")
- **Desire for more free time:** These days, many people feel an emotional guilt about working too much and spending too little time with friends and family. (Example: "Now you can wash your car in half the time.")
- **Feeling of guilt:** Guilt can come in many forms and can be an effective way to move customers to action. Nonprofit organizations often appeal to the emotional trigger of guilt. (Example: "For the

cost of one cup of coffee per day, you could feed a hungry child for a year.")

- **Desire for trust:** Many consumers are looking to buy from a company that has a reputation of integrity. In fact, these consumers might be willing to pay a higher price if they feel a business is trustworthy. (Example: "You'll get an honest estimate with no hidden charges.")
- **Desire to belong to a group:** Customers often buy products to help them feel like a member of a larger group. That group could give them a sense of family, friendship, or simply a broad sense of belonging. (Example: "You're part of the family at Mama's Diner.")
- **Desire to get a good deal and sufficient value in return for money spent:** Many customers are wary of salespeople and businesses thinking they need to find the best deal available before making a purchase. (Example: "If you find a better price for the same product, we'll match it.")

There are countless emotional triggers for different purchases. Think about your product and what emotions prompt customers to purchase it. What are the benefits of your product that appeal to these emotions? This is the last step in developing a comprehensive list of features and benefits. Remember, most people merely glance at an ad and keep going (this behavior will be discussed in further detail in Chapter 6). Something needs to catch their attention and prompt them to stop and take a second look at the ad. Using descriptive language to sell the benefits of your product as well as appealing to your customers' emotions will help you create successful copy.

EXAMPLES OF *FEATURE VS. BENEFIT* COPYWRITING

The easiest way to make sense of features and benefits used in copywriting is through examples. Following are some examples of product features and related benefits to help you get started with a list for your own product or service.

Product: Smooth Lite Beer
Feature: low in carbohydrates
Benefits: helps customers keep off unwanted pounds
Audience: women ages 21–35

To explain further, imagine an ad that simply says, "Drink Smooth Lite Beer. It's low in carbs." You'd probably think that's great but wouldn't jump off your couch to go buy some Smooth Lite Beer. However, imagine the same ad with copy that says, "Put your scale away! Drink low-carb Smooth Lite Beer and avoid those unwanted pounds without sacrificing the taste you love." Customers will hear the new copy and understand Smooth Lite Beer will help them stay thin while still allowing them to have a drink they enjoy. The copy now highlights the benefits of the product and is far more compelling and more likely to appeal to customers who want to drink beer but are afraid of the extra pounds it brings.

Product: Green Lawn Care—residential lawn service
Feature: treats lawns with weed repellent
Benefit: keeps customers' lawns weed free
Audience: homeowners

Imagine an ad that says, "Green Lawn Care applies weed repellent to your lawn." Your initial reaction upon hearing this would be that it's great. Now let's change the copy to highlight the benefit instead of the feature by saying, "Choose Green Lawn Care, and you'll never see another weed again." The copy could go on to call attention to other benefits and emotional triggers like having a beautiful lawn that looks like a luxurious carpet, much to the envy of the neighborhood. Customers will understand that if they use Green Lawn Care, life will be easier (no weekend weeding) and better (pride in their homes). Again, the important thing to remember is that your ad needs to show how your product benefits customers. Don't just list your product's features and hope your customers draw the right conclusions. Spell it out for them!

Product: Healthy-U Vitamins
Feature: contains Biotin
Benefit: makes hair healthier
Audience: teens and young women

An ad that only highlights features for this product might say, "Healthy-U Vitamins include biotin." Most customers have no idea how biotin will help them, so simply mentioning this feature does nothing to create a perceived need for it or Healthy-U Vitamins. Now look at copy for the same product that calls attention to the product's benefits, not the related feature, "Your hair will grow fuller, shinier, and healthier than ever before thanks to a special ingredient in Healthy-U Vitamins called biotin." The new copy tells customers they will develop gorgeous hair by using Healthy-U Vitamins.

 ## REAL-WORLD EXAMPLES

Some famous advertising campaigns have done amazing jobs of turning product features into benefits. In fact, an important benefit can be turned into an entire advertising campaign. Think of the Timex commercials from many years ago that featured the copy, "Takes a licking and keeps on ticking." Timex cleverly turned a feature of their watches (durable) into a useful benefit (you won't have to spend money or time to get a new watch anytime soon). Years ago, watches didn't last forever. This copy focused on a benefit customers wanted—buying a watch that would last no matter what the owner did to it.

Another great example of benefits copywriting comes from a well-known advertising campaign that includes a clever concept tie-in. The pink Energizer Bunny with copy that says, "It keeps going and going and going . . ." demonstrates a subtle and effective way to hype a product's benefits through clever copywriting and a concept that enhances the copy. The feature (and differentiator) of Energizer batteries is that they last a long time—longer than the competitors' batteries. The benefit is that users won't have to worry about their children's toys or other battery operated items dying after a short amount of use. The copy gives them peace of mind that their items will continue working for a long, long time, which equates to a stronger sense of security, fewer trips to the store, and less out-of-pocket money for batteries.

Recently, I saw a print ad for the Nissan Altima with copy that read, "Envy. Terrible to feel. Wonderful to provoke." This copy provides a great example of appealing to emotional triggers. It addresses the need customers have to be trendy or cool as well as the need to keep up with the competition. The ad goes on to list a variety of features of the car and says, "Suddenly, you're the one that's turning heads." The copy successfully appeals to the target audience's perceived need by hyping the benefit to this highly interested and motivated group of customers.

SUMMARY

Large companies with big advertising budgets can afford to invest money on clever, subtle benefits copy. However, small business owners with limited advertising budgets most likely have to decide if money is better spent on straightforward copywriting that leaves no room for guesswork or on clever, creative copy. It's important to see the difference and know that both methods have their useful and appropriate places in the copywriting world. For example, I saw a print ad for Secret antiperspirant with copy that simply said, "My Secret, I sweat more than my boyfriend," and nothing else. This copy might work for a well-known brand like Secret, but I would not recommend it for a small or medium-size business. While it implies a benefit of Secret, it does not *explicitly* communicate any information about benefits or provide any other compelling reason to try Secret antiperspirant. When your advertising budget is limited, it's essential that your copy leaves no room for guesswork or misinterpretation by your customers. It's your job to tell your customers what they need to know to respond to your ad in the way you want.

CASE STUDY ABC TAX SERVICES

Each step of the Copywriting Outline is followed by a case study based on a fictitious company, ABC Tax Services, which demonstrates the process of building an outline at a high level. Chapter 17 provides the entire Copywriting Outline sample for ABC Tax Services as well as ad and marketing collateral samples showing how the elements of the Copywriting Outline can be used to create effective copy.

Copywriting Outline Step 1

Step 1: Exploit Your Product's Benefits—How is my product better than other similar products available (i.e., the competition)? Why is my product the best?

- **Feature:** Trained tax preparers
  - **Benefit:** With our tax preparers, errors are less likely to appear on your return. You'll have peace of mind that your return will be processed smoothly and your refund will arrive quickly. Emotional triggers = trust and instant gratification.
  - **Benefit:** We'll find every deduction to maximize your refund. Emotional trigger = desire to get a good deal.
- **Feature:** Provide e-file services
  - **Benefit:** You'll get your refund fast because your return will be immediately sent to the IRS, rather than in days or weeks by snail mail. Emotional trigger = instant gratification.
- **Feature:** Ten member staff with six tax preparers, one computer technician, two receptionists, and one mail clerk
  - **Benefit:** Our large staff means your business and questions will be addressed quickly; however, we are small enough to know who you are when you call. You get one-on-one, personal service every time you stop by or call, and you're treated like our top priority. Emotional triggers = instant gratification.
- **Feature:** Provide audit protection service
  - **Benefit:** If your return is flagged for an audit, one of our tax preparers will help you navigate through the communications with the IRS until the audit is over. Emotional trigger = trust.

The first step of the Copywriting Outline is the most difficult and time consuming, but it is also the foundation of all your future copywriting projects. Take your time and be as comprehensive as possible. Most importantly, put yourself in your customers' shoes and determine what you would want or need your product to do for you as a customer. Then turn these needs and desires into compelling benefits.

As you work your way through Step 1, don't worry if you can't think of a benefit for every feature on your list. The Copywriting Outline is a work in progress, meaning it's an ever-changing tool. It will never be complete, and it will never be perfect. Remember, it's not Shakespeare. Allow yourself time to learn and improve as you go. Most importantly, don't be intimidated. Tackling the first step of the Copywriting Outline is a major achievement for the nonprofessional copywriter. Applaud yourself for a job well done and get ready for Step 2.

chapter four

step two
Exploit Your Competition's Weaknesses

RESEARCH AND UNDERSTAND YOUR COMPETITION

Step 2 of the Copywriting Outline can be the most enjoyable part of developing the copywriting plan for your product. It is your chance to put into words why your competition is completely inferior to you. Have fun, but proceed with caution.

To write compelling copy, it is essential that you know what differentiates your product from the competition. Once you know your competitors' weaknesses, you must make sure your audience knows them and understands why buying your competitors' products would be a terrible mistake. Get started by thoroughly researching your competition and understanding what they offer in terms of products and services. Next, list the elements of their offerings that are inferior to your own. Feel free to tear the competition apart but be realistic in your comparisons. You want to be able to support your claims if you are challenged.

LEARNING OBJECTIVES

How to research your competitors and find differentiators

■

How to quantify and communicate differentiators

■

How to use customer testimonials and expert opinions

■

How to create hard and soft differentiators

Additionally, as part of your competitor analysis, you need to take the time to investigate how they react to challenges. For example, if you launch an advertising campaign stating that your prices are the lowest available, will your competition likely follow suit by dropping their prices to match or beat yours? If so, your advertising campaign will be outdated and inaccurate before you have a chance to earn a return on your investment. You must determine your ultimate advertising goals and then create copy that will help you meet these goals. Don't be short-sighted by ignoring the reaction of your competition. Not only should you evaluate previous responses your competitors made to market changes, but you should also theorize on how they will react to the steps you take to market your business and products in the future. Most companies will counter an attack. From the start, learn to expect a response from your competition and craft your marketing campaign and corresponding copy in ways that consider this reaction.

To be successful, you must always know what your competition is doing.

AVOID GIVING FREE PUBLICITY TO YOUR COMPETITORS

There are two schools of thought related to mentioning your competitors in your advertising and marketing copy. The first school believes you should never mention your competitors by name, while the second school believes that mentioning your competitors does not negatively impact the effectiveness of your advertising investment. I belong to the first school of thought.

First, the reason for not mentioning your competitors in your copy is simple. Why give your competitors free publicity, and why give them an opportunity to respond with a counterattack? Second, depending on the type of business you're promoting in your copy, many consumers might not even know who your competitors are. Why would you want to tell potential customers about your competitors' products or services? Don't give your customers the opportunity to research your competitor and learn what they have to offer. When you write copy, you want the audience to think about the business, product, and service being advertised and not the other options in the marketplace. Take some time to evaluate both schools of thought before determining whether or not you want to mention your competitors in your copy.

QUANTIFY YOUR DIFFERENTIATORS

If you can quantify the differences between your product and your competitor's product, you've hit the jackpot. For example, if your competitor only offers a one-year guarantee on their product, but you offer a five-year guarantee, shout it to the world in your copy. In Step 4 of the Copywriting Outline, I'll show you how to personalize your copy to effectively sell this difference to your customers, but in Step 2, just list the differences between you and your competitors and quantify them whenever possible. Nothing helps draw attention to the differences between products better than hard numbers. There are so many ways to quantify the differences between you and your competition. Get creative and have fun with it. Following is a list of differentiators that are easily quantifiable:

- Selection
- Price
- Store hours
- Customer service hours
- Delivery hours
- Delivery rates
- Parking availability
- Location
- Number of employees available and dedicated to customers' needs
- Free tie-ins: For example, some camera stores include batteries with a new camera purchase, which is a nice savings to customers that is not offered by all stores.

LET EXPERT OPINIONS WORK FOR YOU

Another effective way to differentiate your product from the competition is through published reports or expert opinions. If there is an organization or expert affiliated with your line of business who has published articles or interviews related to your product or service, you may be able to use that information in your copy. For example, imagine the Association of Carpet Cleaners (a fictitious organization) published a report stating that using XYZ Stain Remover along with 123 Cleaner is the most effective way to remove red wine stains from carpets. Now let's say that Joe's Carpet Cleaning uses this method to remove stains, but Joe's competitor, Bob's Carpet Cleaning, uses an older cleaning method and solution. This is the perfect opportunity for Joe to significantly differentiate his business from his competition. Now the consumer will think, "It's not just Joe telling me his cleaning service is better than Bob's, but the Association of Carpet Cleaners says so, too." While Bob's method of removing wine stains from carpets still works very well, Joe has an authoritative source to help differentiate his service in his customers' minds.

Ask your customers for testimonials. You'll be surprised how many will be happy to help and share their opinions.

Obtaining expert opinions and testimonials related directly to you, your business, and your product is also an excellent resource for future copywriting initiatives. If you don't have any expert opinions or testimonials, don't worry. Getting them is as simple as asking your customers for testimonials and your business associates for expert opinions. For example, an expert opinion could come from an organization or group to which you belong, and a testimonial could come from one of your best customers. Expert opinions are always the most compelling when you can tie an important organization or title to the person providing them, while testimonials are most effective when you include a picture of the customer who provided the comment in your marketing materials. Expert opinions and customer testimonials from anonymous sources are often meaningless to consumers because they wonder if they are even legitimate. For opinions and testimonials to add value to your copy, they need to come from verifiable sources. It's also important to remember to obtain written permission to use a customer's or expert's words and likeness in your copy.

THE DIFFERENCE BETWEEN HARD AND SOFT DIFFERENTIATORS

Frequently, you will not be able to quantify a key differentiator between your product and the competition. Don't be afraid to get creative to communicate subjective points to your customers. For example, many products are very price sensitive and demand increases with a drop in prices or decreases when prices rise. In economics terminology, these products are considered "elastic," meaning price has a strong effect on sales. Other differentiators are often secondary when it comes to a customer's buying decision. Products whose demand is not affected by price changes (including most necessities) are considered "inelastic." Milk is a perfect example of an inelastic product. Most people are not sensitive to where they buy their milk, and prices don't vary drastically from one store to another. Convenience is one of the few strong differentiators in terms of a milk purchasing decision (i.e., the location of the store). How else can the store owner differentiate himself to draw in more customers? One way is to create soft differentiators.

Unlike a hard differentiator that is easily quantifiable and proven, a soft differentiator is more subjective. For example, differentiating cheese can be challenging, so the California Milk Producers Advisory Board created copy to advertise Real California Cheese that said, "Great cheese comes from happy cows, and happy cows come from California." The copy was supported by clever commercial concepts that helped attract the attention of the audience. Who knew that cheese from happy cows is better than from depressed cows? No one, until Real California Cheese made customers *think* there was a difference by creating a soft differentiator.

Differentiating yourself from your competition is critical and including hard and soft differentiators in your copy will make your ads more compelling and effective. As I'll discuss in further detail in Step 9 of the Copy-writing Outline, be sure you can prove your claims when comparing your product or service to the competition. Most importantly, be relentless in your research of the competition. A critical component to your product's success is being aware of the marketplace, including your competition. Staying current on the changes in your competition's business and products will allow you to capitalize on potential differentiators in future copywriting projects. Having that knowledge will put you in the driver's seat where you can proactively launch marketing campaigns and corresponding copy from a position of control rather than simply reacting to your competitors' actions.

> As you research your competitors, they're researching you. Be prepared to respond to competitive attacks against you.

ATTACK THE NEGATIVES

If your business or product does have negative features associated with it, don't try to hide them. Instead, attack them head on. It's inevitable that your competitors will use your weakness as a way to differentiate their businesses from yours, and they will undoubtedly promote that differentiator as a benefit of choosing their products or services. Before your competitors have the chance to create a message targeted to your weakness, find a way to turn your weakness into a positive. If you can't find a way to turn your weakness into a copywriting opportunity, it may be time to reevaluate that part of your business and make the necessary changes, so you can stay competitive in the eyes of consumers.

EXAMPLES OF *COMPETITIVE DIFFERENTIATOR* COPYWRITING

Following are examples of copywriting that focus on differentiators to give you some ideas of how you can exploit your competition's weaknesses.

Product: Kids Taste Juice
Differentiator: competitors' juices contain more sugar

The owners of Kids Taste Juice know their product is healthier than competing products. They need to use effective copywriting to draw attention to this differentiator and make sure customers understand why the product is healthier. Rather than simply saying, "Kids Taste Juice contains only 60% sugar," the copy needs to spell out the difference in no uncertain terms. A more compelling copy approach could read, "Kids Taste Juice is made with 20% less sugar than similar juices. Your kids don't need that extra sugar. You can feel good about giving them the *healthier* juice when you pour a glass of Kids Taste Juice." This copy quantifies the difference between Kids Taste Juice and the competition and points out exactly how that differentiator affects a customer in a positive way through a specific benefit (i.e., less sugar for children and a healthier product). The copy makes customers feel good about buying Kids Taste Juice because it taps into customers' feelings of guilt about giving their children a drink that is unhealthy.

To further explain, "Kids Taste Juice contains only 60% sugar" states the amount of sugar in the juice. This may be a commendable statistic but out of context it is not useful to the audience. However, when the copy draws a direct comparison to the competition and highlights a quantifiable differentiator ("Kids Taste Juice is made with 20% less sugar than similar juices. Your kids don't need that extra sugar. You can feel good about giving them the *healthier* juice when you pour a glass of Kids Taste Juice."), it takes on a new level of importance to the audience. Now they can understand that Kids Taste Juice is better than other juices in a specific area, which is undoubtedly very important to parents. When writing copy, it is important to understand how your product is different from the competition and turn those differentiators into compelling copy points that relate directly to your customers.

Product: Bug-Be-Gone Exterminators—residential extermination services
Differentiator: length of guarantee

Again, when you know your product is better than your competitors' product and you can quantify it, shout it to the world. If you offer a six-month guarantee on your services but your competition only offers a three-month guarantee, make sure your customers know about that difference. Then tell them how that difference will affect them personally. For example, instead of saying, "Our work is guaranteed for six months," show your customers that your competitors don't offer this guarantee. A more effective use of copy to sell this differentiator might say, "Unlike other exterminators who only stand behind their work for three months, we'll guarantee you won't see another bug for the next six months." Which copy version is more compelling and would motivate you to act? The second version is more effective because it tells the customer that choosing the competitor is a mistake while personalizing the benefits of getting Bug-Be-Gone Exterminators' special service guarantee.

Product: Everything Appliances—kitchen appliances
Differentiator: free delivery and installation

Delivery and installation services are great ways to differentiate your business from the competition. First, these differentiators are quantifiable. You can show customers how much money they'll save by choosing your product instead of competitors' products. There is perhaps no greater motivator in purchasing decisions than saving money. Make sure your customers know the benefits of free delivery and installation vs. other delivery and installation offers. Instead of saying, "We offer free delivery and installation," personalize the service for your customers. Your copy could say, "You'll spend up to $100 for delivery and installation at other appliance stores, but when you shop at Everything Appliances, you can keep that money in your pocket because all deliveries are free." Which copy would motivate you more? You can't assume customers can interpret your copy. It's up to you to ensure they understand it, and they are motivated to act on it.

Product: José's Gas Station—gasoline
Differentiator: clean

Gas is an inelastic product; customers generally buy gas regardless of the price, and the major differentiator is typically convenience (primarily in terms of location). The owner of José's Gas Station could further differentiate his business by creating a soft differentiator based on the cleanliness of his station. Knowing most gas stations are not very clean, the owner could make an effort to ensure that his gas station is clean and a pleasure to visit. Copy could drive this point home to customers by saying, "Make your next pit stop at José's Gas Station—guaranteed to be as clean as your own home (even the bathrooms)." This copy points out the differentiator and appeals to a customer's emotional trigger of the desire for comfort. Everyone wants to be comfortable and feel like they're at home when they're traveling. This copy feeds that desire and challenges a traditional assumption that most gas station bathrooms are dirty.

 REAL-WORLD EXAMPLES

There are many famous ads that focus on product differentiation. All advertisers and business owners want to show customers how their products are better than their competitors' products. The marketing team behind Hefty Garbage Bags hit a home run in product differentiation advertising with their "Hefty, hefty, hefty. Wimpy, wimpy, wimpy," campaign. Just six words of copy tell a complete story. Hefty Garbage Bags are stronger than other garbage bags. Sounds great. It's simple, in-your-face copywriting that tells customers in no uncertain terms why Hefty Garbage bags are better than other garbage bags.

Another example is Johnson's Baby Shampoo and their ad copy that promises, "No more tears." Not only does this differentiate Johnson's Baby Shampoo from their competition but it also creates a great benefit for customers. Johnson's Baby Shampoo will not sting their children's eyes. What parent wants their child to cry during bathing and shampooing? This copy leverages the emotional feeling of providing comfort and security as well as the trigger of guilt. First, parents want their children to feel loved and secure, but at the same time, they feel guilty when parental requirements (like shampooing) cause their children to be unhappy. Johnson's Baby Shampoo solves all of these problems, and the copy clearly communicates the benefits to consumers who choose to purchase Johnson's Baby Shampoo over competitors' products.

One of the best ad campaigns that focused on differentiating a company and product from the competition was created for Saturn. When General Motors launched their Saturn division, its whole purpose was to provide a different kind of car-buying experience for customers. No longer would customers have to haggle over prices and wonder if they were being taken advantage of or getting a great deal. With Saturn, prices are final and cars are safe. Copy in their famous ad campaign said, "A different kind of company. A different kind of car." This was a message customers were longing to hear, and they responded. Customers trusted Saturn and appreciated the company's honesty. By focusing their copy on key differentiators and emotional triggers, Saturn built a solid brand image and boosted sales in the 1990s.

SUMMARY

Take some time to research your competitors thoroughly as you work through Step 2 of the Copywriting Outline. Define the hard and soft differ-

CASE STUDY ABC TAX SERVICES

See Chapter 17 for the complete Copywriting Outline for ABC Tax Services as well as ad and marketing collateral samples using copy culled from the Copywriting Outline.

Copywriting Outline Step 2

Step 2: Exploit Your Competition's Weaknesses—How are my competitors' products inferior to mine?

- They offer no peace-of-mind guarantee. ABC Tax Services provides a Confidence Guarantee that no other tax preparer can beat. If you receive a refund that is different from what ABC Tax Services quotes, ABC Tax Services will refund the difference (up to 10%, excluding withholdings for IRS or medical debt or other liens against the refund). *Notice how the guarantee was branded as a Confidence Guarantee to further appeal to consumers' desire for trust and security.*

- They employ tax preparers who are not members of the National Association of Tax Practitioners. You can rest assured that your tax return will be prepared accurately because every tax preparer at ABC Tax Services has passed stringent testing requirements set by the National Association of Tax Practitioners. That's just one more way ABC Tax Services helps you safely navigate the tax maze.

- They offer no audit assistance. If your tax return is flagged for an audit, you won't be left alone. A representative from ABC Tax Services will work with you to navigate the audit process from start to finish.

- They charge for e-filing. ABC Tax Services will e-file your tax return for free, so you'll get your refund fast and at no extra charge.

- They don't have a live answering service. ABC Tax Services is here when you need help. A representative answers our phones 24 hours per day, which means you can call us any time you need us. Don't wait until tomorrow morning. Call now!

entiators between you and your competition and then quantify those differentiators wherever possible. This is one of the most enjoyable steps of the Copywriting Outline, so have fun with it. However, it is critical that you are able to substantiate the claims you make in your copy, particularly those you make against your competitors, so tread carefully. An effective way to support your claims is through customer testimonials and expert opinions. Don't be afraid to ask for them.

Once you've completed Step 2 of the Copywriting Outline and thoroughly torn your competition apart, take a moment to congratulate yourself on finishing the most challenging part of any copywriting project. Steps 1 and 2 of the Copywriting Outline lay the groundwork for all of your future copywriting projects. Make sure your work is comprehensive, then take a breath and get ready to turn your product's features, benefits, and differentiators into compelling, action-oriented copy in the next steps of your Copywriting Outline.

chapter five

step three
Know Your Audience

BEFORE YOU WRITE YOUR AD, PLACE YOUR AD

Every person in the world is not going to see every ad in the world. Each ad has a specific audience who will see it, and it's the marketer's job to find the best placement to ensure the target audience will see it. For example, an ad for skateboards placed in a local senior citizen housing association newsletter is not likely to generate a lot of sales. In fact, it would be a waste of advertising dollars. The target audience for skateboards is teenagers or young adults. The vast majority of senior citizens do not use skateboards, and it is not a product category in which they typically purchase gifts. Before you buy ad space, make sure you're spending your money in the right place to get the biggest bang for your buck in terms of exposure and building awareness of your product or service.

First, take the time to research your customers thoroughly. In most businesses, 20% of customers are responsible for 80% of sales (this is called the

LEARNING OBJECTIVES

How to find your best customers

How to create a demographic profile of your customers

How to segment your customers into groups with similar characteristics

How to change the tone of your copy to match your audience

80/20 rule in case you're curious about the official marketing terminology for this phenomenon). That 20% represents your best customer, and your job is to determine who that 20% is. Evaluate your customers and put together a demographic profile of your most valuable customer, so you can advertise in the best places to find similar people who are likely prospects. If you're a small business owner, you probably don't have a budget set aside to conduct a thorough research study and analysis of your customer base, so you'll have to improvise by using your own communication skills and visual investigation. Remember, you're trying to develop a *basic* profile of your target customer, not a CIA profile of each individual who buys your product. Do your best with the information you have.

Segmenting your customers includes learning how different customers use your product and the various benefits customers derive from those different uses.

There are many attributes you can use to develop a demographic profile of your customers. Following is a list of examples of traits to help you start your own demographic profiling initiative:

- **Gender:** This demographic is usually fairly easy to detect visually.
- **Age:** You can estimate your customers' ages based on their appearances.
- **Ethnicity:** You can guess your customers' ethnicities based on their appearances.
- **Family status:** Take note of who your customers are shopping with and what they're carrying. Do they have children with them? Do they appear married?
- **Income:** Notice your customers' clothing, purses, wallets, cars, cell phones, etc. While appearance can be deceiving in terms of income, it may be the only thing you have to work with when trying to define the income level of your target audience.

- **Occupation:** This demographic can be determined through conversation. Act like you're making small talk, when in fact, you have an underlying motive to develop your target audience's demographic profile. Talking with customers will also give you an opportunity to develop relationships with them, which will help drive customer loyalty as we will discuss in Chapter 14. It also may give you a chance to ask for a customer testimonial as we discussed in Chapter 4.
- **Interests:** You can determine your customers' interests through conversations or visual investigation. Your customer might be wearing a baseball T-shirt or carrying an "I love to cook" key chain.

Once the profile is complete, you can use it to segment your customers into groups with similar characteristics. You can create marketing campaigns with unique copy for a specific target audience based on the demographic segmentation you complete in Step 3 of the Copywriting Outline. Additionally, you can determine which customer segment is most likely to buy your product. Then, you'll need to research your local advertising opportunities and pick the newspapers, newsletters, radio stations, etc. where your message is most likely to reach your target audience for each ad or marketing campaign.

Even the best copy can't help boost sales if the right people aren't seeing the ad. For example, if you're selling house cleaning services, your target audience might include both working parents who are too busy to clean their homes *and* senior citizens who are not physically capable of cleaning their homes. When your research is complete and you determine the profile of your most valuable customers, place your ad in media those customers are likely to see. Once you know where you're going to place your ad, you can develop copy that speaks to your specific target audience. Understanding your medium will be discussed in further detail in Chapter 8.

The demographic possibilities are endless. Be observant and you'll be surprised at what you can learn simply by closely looking at your customers. It's also important to note that you should write each ad or marketing message to hype the benefits that are most important to the specific target audience meant to see or hear it. In fact, you may even want to build awareness among a new target audience where you think you can generate sales, but your product is not known yet. Remember, the Copywriting Outline is a working document, and conducting demographic research and segmenting customers isn't a one-time activity. Instead, continually observe and analyze your customers, so you always understand who they are and what they want and need. Tailor your copy to appeal to the specific target audience for your marketing initiatives to maximize your return on investment. With that in mind, the next challenge is writing compelling copy that will motivate the target audience who sees your ad to buy your product.

WRITE COPY FOR THE RIGHT PEOPLE

A copywriter cannot write compelling copy if he or she does not know the target audience. A targeted ad or marketing campaign requires specific copywriting created exclusively for the audience who is meant to read, see, or hear it. It is essential that you understand the targeted group of customers for each ad or marketing piece so you can develop messages they will understand and relate to and ultimately drive them to action. To create compelling copy that speaks to your target audience, you need to know how to find them (i.e., place your ad appropriately) and what to say to them. Step 3 of the Copywriting Outline is when you will need to use your demographic profile to write sample phrases, sentences, and paragraphs that speak to the needs, desires, and emotional triggers for each of your target audiences. You need to gain an understanding of your target audiences' hot buttons and then your copy needs to push those buttons.

Understanding your audience can make or break your marketing and advertising campaigns.

For example, a florist has a variety of target audiences, and each audience has a very different set of needs and hot buttons. Customers who purchase flowers to celebrate the birth of a baby have very different hot buttons than

CLOSEUP

The Four Rights of Advertising
1. Right message to the
2. Right audience at the
3. Right time in the
4. Right place

customers who purchase flowers to grieve a death. As a result, these two audiences require very different copy to motivate them to pick up the phone and call a florist's shop to place their floral delivery order. Remember, every demographic group or segment of your customer base has specific needs. Your copy needs to communicate the right message to the right group at the right time and in the right place to be successful. I call this the Four Rights of Advertising. (See Closeup Box.)

MATCH YOUR TONE TO YOUR AUDIENCE

Remember, understanding your audience can make or break your copy. When you're writing copy, you need to change your tone and words depending on your audience, just like when you're having a conversation with someone. Most likely, you change your tone and words when you're speaking with your boss vs. your spouse or child. While you might say to your boss, "I utilized a best practice methodology to develop my innovative strategy," you would probably not use those words or that professional tone when you speak with your friends or family. Instead, you might say, "I had a great idea today," when speaking to your family. The same concept holds true in copywriting. Knowing your audience and writing copy that speaks directly to them will compel them to action and drive them to buy your product or service.

EXAMPLES OF COPYWRITING FOR A *SPECIFIC TARGET AUDIENCE*

The following examples will show you how to rewrite copy so it speaks to a specific target audience.

Product: Stylez Jeans
Target Audience: teens and young women

In this example, assume Ann's company sells Stylez Jeans and her target audience is young women who read fashion magazines. She discovered that these characteristics are typical of her target audience through her demographic research and resulting profile. More than likely, she determined their age through appearance, and perhaps, she saw a trend that her most valuable customers were carrying fashion magazines or referring to them in conversations with Ann or their shopping companions. Also, assume she has chosen to place her ad in the local dance and gymnastics school's monthly newsletter.

Ann could include copy in her ad highlighting a key feature—the durability of Stylez Jeans, "Top quality denim lets Stylez Jeans stand up to your toughest use and abuse." While durability is a great feature for jeans, would this copy speak to young women? What do young women want out of their clothes? Typically, they want to look and feel good in their clothes. A better copy approach would read, "With the high-quality, designer denim fabric of Stylez Jeans, your legs will look slim and beautiful." By changing the copy to highlight an audience-appropriate feature and corresponding benefit, it speaks directly to the target customer group.

If the target audience for these jeans was men working in construction, a different benefit, like durability, as well as a different medium to place the ad would be more appropriate. Pick the features that are important to your target audience and then focus on the benefits of those features in your copy. By speaking directly to your customers in this way, you'll give them the information they need to act and buy your product.

Product: Maria's Accounting Services—tax return preparation
Target Audience: small business owners

In this example, assume that Maria's Accounting Services is advertising in the local paper to generate business from small business owners during the tax season. Maria's demographic research shows that small business owners have unique tax situations and often need help preparing their taxes. Maria wants to expand her business within this target audience, so she could use copy that says, "Maria's Accounting Services gets your tax refund back fast." It's great that Maria's Accounting Services is fast and customers get their tax refunds quickly, but since most small business owners are sole proprietors who usually have a balance due on their tax returns, hyping her speedy refund service is not Maria's best tactic to motivate her target audience. Instead, she could say, "Make sure you don't miss any deductions. Visit Maria's Accounting Services and ease the pain of taxes." The copy now addresses the needs of her target audience who typically have difficult tax returns and a balance due that can only be reduced by finding every possible deduction. It also focuses on a key benefit (lowering the customer's tax liability) and an emotional trigger (peace of mind by easing the pain of taxes).

Product: Florida Roofers—roofing repairs and installation
Target Audience: mobile home owners with metal roofs

After a series of severe hurricanes swept the Florida coast, Florida Roofers decided to try to break into the mobile home market, which includes many homes with metal roofs, because they recognized that there was growth potential beyond their traditional shingle roofing services. The owner, Dion, purchased ad space in an upcoming newsletter for one of the largest mobile home developments in his area. He could use the following copy, "Florida Roofers has over 10 years experience fixing damage to shingle roofs." However, Dion's target audience doesn't have shingle roofs. Mobile homeowners with metal roofs would not be compelled to contact Florida Roofers based on hearing that the company has experience fixing shingle roofs. If Dion uses copy that says, "Florida Roofers will fix your metal roof fast with the same quality that has kept our customers happy for over 10 years," his copy speaks directly to the sense of urgency homeowners feel after a storm damages their roofs, and it also helps them feel confident that Florida Roofers will do the job right. The copy focuses on both the emotional triggers of trust and instant gratification.

 ## REAL-WORLD EXAMPLES

Flip through your TV channels and watch the commercials on each channel. You'll see how companies change the tone of their copywriting to appeal to the audience who is most likely watching the program on that station at any given time. For example, if you turn on the Disney channel, you'll undoubtedly see a lot of toy commercials. However, if you turn on ESPN, you'll probably see a lot of car commercials. Not only will the products advertised vary based on the channel and corresponding audience, but the messages will change as well.

McDonald's provides a perfect real-world example of changing messages to relate to different target audiences. If you turn on MTV, a channel that caters to teenagers, you'll see McDonald's ads inviting viewers to visit "Mickey D's," while a McDonald's commercial on The Discovery Channel, which caters to an older target audience, refers to the restaurant by its full name, "McDonald's." It's a subtle but very effective change that helps the copy speak directly to the target audience in terms in which they can relate.

American Express provides another great example of changing an ad and the copy that goes along with it to appeal to different audiences. Over the past several years, American Express has used an ad campaign that says, "My life. My card." Each ad focuses on a celebrity describing how he or she uses an American Express card to match each celebrity's individual lifestyle. Not only does this ad campaign successfully personalize the benefits of the American Express card, but it also uses celebrities who speak directly to each target audience. For example, Ellen DeGeneres, Jerry Seinfeld, and Shawn White have each appeared in an American Express ad, and each appeals to a different audience. An American Express ad in a snowboarding magazine that features Shawn White (Olympic Snowboarding Gold Medalist) and the various ways he uses his American Express card appeals more to readers of that magazine than the same ad featuring Ellen DeGeneres. Snowboarders are likely to see how Shawn White uses his American Express card and not only think they need to get an American Express card to be like him, but they also need to buy some of the same items Shawn White buys with his American Express card. Snowboarders are less likely to be compelled to action when they see the various ways Ellen DeGeneres uses her American Express card. The celebrity and copy were chosen specifically for the target audience that the messages will reach.

Another example comes from a Target commercial that used copy clearly targeted to a female audience. The commercial advertised a new clothing line at Target stores, and the copy said, "Now at prices any goddess can afford." This is a great example of copy that is written to speak to a specific target audience. The same copy would not work well for a Target commercial appearing on ESPN that advertises sporting equipment. In fact, the same copy would not even work well to promote menswear in the same clothing line. On the contrary, this copy is meant for a target audience of women, and it works well for that reason.

 **SUMMARY**

The demographic profile of your target audience is a work in progress. You'll continually find new ways to tweak it to make it as comprehensive and specific

CASE STUDY ABC TAX SERVICES

See Chapter 17 for the complete Copywriting Outline for ABC Tax Services as well as ad and marketing collateral samples using copy culled form the Copywriting Outline.

Copywriting Outline Step 3

Step 3: Know Your Audience—Who should buy my product or who is likely to want or need it (i.e., target audience/market)? Who will see my ad?

- **Target Audience:** Taxpayers expecting a refund
  - Common demographics of target audience:
    - Married
    - Children under 18 years of age
    - Homeowner
    - Age 25–45
    - Income between $30,000–75,000
    - Interests include family activities such as sports, travel, movies, dining out

as possible. Take the time to talk to your customers and ask them why they chose your product or service. While your budget as a small or medium-size business owner may not include wide-scale, quantitative research related to consumer behavior, you can conduct your own qualitative research simply by conversing with your customers and asking them questions to help you build your demographic profile. Listen to your customers and find out what they want or need from your product. Find out what compelled them to action and motivated them to purchase your product or service. Determine the trends that permeate through your target audience and push those hot buttons in your copy.

Finally, put yourself in your customers' shoes. If someone tells you something that has little or no effect on your life, you probably either barely listen to or completely ignore the person talking to you. The same concept holds true with copywriting. If the copy doesn't affect customers' lives, they won't pay attention to the ad. However, if the copy pushes their hot buttons and speaks directly to their needs, desires, and emotional triggers, they'll stop, listen, and act thereby boosting your sales and profits.

chapter six

step four
Communicate W.I.F.M. (What's In It For Me?)

KNOW THE PURPOSE OF YOUR AD OR MARKETING PIECE

There are a variety of reasons to create an advertisement or marketing piece. Before you write copy for your promotional piece, you need to understand your goals for that piece. What do you want to get in return? The copy you use in each ad or marketing piece will vary based on your goals for that promotion. While this book does not focus on the development of marketing plans and strategies, I will offer some examples of different objectives for ads or marketing pieces that, in turn, will affect the copy you use:

- **Communicate a special offer:** Retailers frequently want to communicate a special offer to customers to boost short-term store traffic.
- **Share information and raise awareness:** Medical offices often want to share infor-

LEARNING OBJECTIVES

How to match your copy to the specific purpose of your ads and marketing pieces

■

How to speak directly to your customers' needs in your copy

■

How to use the SLAP Test to analyze the effectiveness of your copy

mation with current and potential customers about a new procedure or medication to build awareness of the service.

- **Generate leads:** Realtors commonly use promotional pieces such as ads or direct mail to promote their services and generate inquiries from prospective clients.

There are many reasons why businesses choose to place an advertisement, issue a press release, create a marketing brochure, send a direct mail piece, or execute another marketing tactic. As the advertiser, you need to determine up-front why you are creating your marketing piece and then develop copy that will help you reach the goals for that piece. For example, if you are a retailer with an excessive amount of stock of an item, you might want to discount the price and advertise that discount as a short-term sale. Alternatively, you could offer that item for free with every purchase over a predetermined dollar amount or offer a completely different popular item for free or at a discounted price if a customer buys the sale item. These are just a few examples of promotions that can be used to help a retailer reduce overstock of a product. The role of the copy used in the corresponding marketing piece is to communicate the promotion in a way that speaks directly to the target audience and motivates them to action. In other words, the copy needs to include the right message to persuade the customer to make a purchase, thereby meeting the retailer's goal for the promotion and corresponding marketing piece.

At the end of the day, every business that invests money into creating, producing, and running an advertisement has a goal for that ad, which includes generating a specific return on the investment. Copywriting is an integral part of meeting those goals. Remember, it's the copy that communicates the message and convinces the customer to act. With that in mind, your copy needs to speak to your intended audience to generate the response and return required from the advertising or marketing investment.

TELL YOUR CUSTOMERS EXACTLY HOW YOU CAN HELP THEM

Your customers need to understand how your product or service is going to help them by making their lives easier, making them feel better, helping them save money, helping them save time, etc. In Step 4 of the Copywriting Outline, you'll build on the work you've done so far by taking your product's features, benefits, and differentiators and *specifically* describing how they *directly* affect your target audience members' lives in positive ways. Remember the first tenet of copywriting discussed in Chapter 1—*your product or service is far less important than its ability to fulfill your customers' needs.* Keep this rule in mind as you develop Step 4 of your Copywriting Outline because it will help you write copy that focuses on your customers' needs rather than on you and your product.

Each ad or marketing piece provides a certain amount of real estate to communicate your messages. Use that space wisely and don't waste it.

The first step in communicating directly with your target audience is to capture their attention. You can do this through the use of headlines. Once you've caught their attention, you need to convince them to keep reading (or listening). When people read, view, or hear advertisements, they're waiting to learn what's in it for them. They'll ask themselves, "What do I get if I buy this product?" Don't make them guess. Tell them specifically how they will benefit from buying your product and what you or your product can do for them.

Answer your target audience's question, "What's in it for me?" Remember, you're paying for your ad space and possibly graphic design, too. Don't waste your money by placing an ad with ineffective copy that does not clearly tell your customers what they'll get by buying your product or service. Large companies with big advertising and marketing budgets can test snappy, cliché headlines and copy in an attempt to find the best way to catch their target audience's attention, but small and medium-size business owners typically have limited budgets. For smaller businesses that only have one chance to communicate their message, copy must be written so the message, including benefits and differentiators, is heard and understood by the target audience. There is no room in a small business owner's advertising budget to risk not getting that specific message across to the right people every time.

To illustrate this concept, I'll refer to an ad I saw in my local paper shortly before Valentine's Day. A hair salon placed an ad with a photo of flowers and copy that merely read, "Roses are red. Violets are blue. Come see us for your new hairdo," followed by the salon's name, address, and phone number. The advertiser even went so far as to pay for a full-color ad. This was a significant investment for a small business owner, and I'll admit that the poem is cute. However, from a copywriting perspective, the poem is completely ineffective and a waste of advertising dollars. I think very few people would be motivated to act and visit this hair salon based on the copy in this ad. It does not provide any benefits to customers or tell them what's in it for them if they choose this hair salon. The copy does not speak to customers' desires and needs. In fact, it doesn't speak directly to customers at all.

Let's take a moment to brainstorm ways that this copy could have been written more effectively. Since the ad was placed just before Valentine's Day and the business owner paid for a full-color ad, it seems like a good opportunity to showcase before and after photos of an actual customer. The copy could say, "Make him drool this Valentine's Day with a new you." Again, the important thing to understand is that when you have a small amount of real estate in a print ad to get your message across, don't waste the space or your money. Use the space wisely to ensure that your investment works for you and brings in sales and revenue.

DON'T MAKE YOUR CUSTOMERS PLAY CONNECT THE DOTS

Customers view an ad for just a few seconds before they move on—unless, that is, something catches their attention. Your copy needs to make it easy for them to see how your product will impact their lives. To draw attention to your copy, use bullet points or callouts that answer the question, "What's in it for me?" These are the key selling points for your audience. Never make the mistake of assuming customers will understand what your copy says. Spell it out for them in no uncertain terms so there is no possible question left in their minds about what your product will do for them.

You've created benefits and differentiators and identified your target audience in Steps 1, 2, and 3 of the Copywriting Outline. Now you need to tie them together in your copy. Don't make your customers connect the dots; do it for them. Your copy needs to show your customers how your product's benefits and differentiators will help them. Appeal to the emotional triggers, desires, and needs of your target audience and show them the added value they'll get by choosing your product. As I said earlier in this chapter, answer their question, "What's in it for me?"

If you have trouble answering "What's in it for me?" a useful method to help you tackle Step 4 of the Copywriting Outline involves working backward. Start by thinking of reasons why customers would *not* choose your product or service. Next, develop ways to convince them otherwise. For example, why would a customer *not* choose to purchase flowers from a particular local florist? Perhaps research by the business owner shows customers are concerned about freshness and quality. The owner of the flower shop could convince potential customers otherwise by saying, "Color Burst Flowers has fresh flowers delivered every day, so you get the most vibrant, stunning, and fragrant floral gifts and arrangements." Now the copy shows customers what's in it for them when they choose Color Burst Floral— gorgeous, fresh arrangements. Their hot buttons and emotional triggers have been pushed, and they are more likely to act.

Let's look at another example. The owner of a handyman service might learn that customers are concerned about the types of employees the service sends to their homes. The owner could use copy that says, "At Home

> Don't assume your audience understands your copy. Leave no room for confusion or guesswork.

Handymen performs an extensive background check on every employee, so you can feel safe letting our workers into your home." The copy now speaks directly to customers' concerns about letting strangers into their homes and mitigates the obstacle.

USE THE SLAP TEST

Throughout this book, I repeatedly mention that small business owners typically have small advertising budgets. As a result, your best copywriting approach requires that you ensure your audience understands your message. You need to slap them in the face with your message, so there is no chance they won't hear it or understand it. This is where I like to use my SLAP test. Simply stated, the SLAP test helps you ensure that your message is received by evaluating it to make sure your readers stop, look, act, and purchase. Let me break the steps down.

- **Stop:** You need to be certain your ad or marketing piece makes your audience stop (i.e., it catches their attention).
- **Look/Listen:** Once your audience has stopped, you need to make them want to look at your ad (i.e., read it or watch it) or listen to it. This is how they'll get your message.
- **Act:** Next, you need to convince your audience to act by calling you or visiting your store or website (i.e., follow your call to action).
- **Purchase:** Finally, you need to motivate your audience to purchase your product or service thereby boosting your sales and profits and helping you meet your return on investment goals.

As you work through your Copywriting Outline and review your final copy, use the SLAP test to ensure your message and design pass with flying colors. If your ad slaps your audience in the face and meets the SLAP test criteria, your campaign will be successful and your sales will rise. It's important to remember that SLAPing your audience in the face is different from

☀ CLOSEUP

The SLAP TEST

1. Stop
2. Look/Listen
3. Act
4. Purchase

beating them over the head. The copywriter's job is to strike an appropriate balance between being attention grabbing and action oriented and being overwhelming and hard-selling. This balance will depend on both your audience and your offer.

EXAMPLES OF *WHAT'S IN IT FOR ME* COPYWRITING

The following examples highlight some of the differences between ineffective copywriting that doesn't address customers' specific needs and copy that tells them exactly what the product or service being advertised can do for them.

Product: Super Frying Pan
Feature: made from nonstick material
Benefit: easy clean up
Audience: busy mothers

Imagine an ad that simply says, "Our frying pan has an innovative nonstick coating." Not only does this copy fail to hype the benefit of the nonstick coating, but it also fails to tell customers what's in it for them when they buy the Super Frying Pan. By changing the copy to include, "You'll never have to scrub a frying pan again," you are telling customers exactly how the special feature of the Super Frying Pan will directly affect their lives. You're also appealing to the emotional trigger of wanting to have more free time. With this copywriting change, your target audience will be more apt to stop, look, act, and purchase (SLAP) because you're speaking directly to their needs.

Product: Miguel's Barber Shop—men's haircuts
Feature: open Sundays
Benefit: convenience
Audience: professional men

The majority of professional men work Monday through Friday and are unable to get a haircut during typical barber shop daytime hours. The fact that Miguel's Barber Shop is open on Sundays is a key differentiator from the competition and offers a great benefit to Miguel's target audience who may otherwise have trouble finding time during the week to get haircuts.

Miguel could advertise with copy that says, "Miguel's Barber Shop, 999-555-4444," and I should mention I have seen an ad exactly like this example in my local paper. Does this ad tell the customer what's in it for them if they choose Miguel's Barber Shop? Is this ad likely to generate traffic and boost sales? My experience tells me that Miguel would not get an adequate bang for his buck with this copy. It fails in every way. For example, it describes no features, benefits, or differentiators. Furthermore, it doesn't speak directly to customers. There is no compelling reason given in the copy to choose Miguel's Barber Shop over any other shop in the area. If Miguel changed his copy to say, "You're busy. That's why Miguel's Barber Shop is open on Sundays," he can highlight his main differentiator and appeal to his customers' emotional triggers of needing more free time. Miguel could elaborate further with key descriptive words including "convenient" and "easy," but the copy above succeeds in catching the busy target audience's attention and giving them a compelling reason to visit Miguel's Barber Shop.

Product: Twice-as-Nice Consignments—used merchandise
Feature: low prices
Benefit: customers save money
Audience: working women

In this example, the owner of Twice-as-Nice Consignments could write copy that says, "Twice-as-Nice Consignments has a wide selection of low-cost, high-quality clothing and home décor." This copy certainly tells customers that Twice-as-Nice Consignments has low prices, and they don't appear to sell junk. Now imagine the copy is changed to say, "Don't pay full price! Everything you'll find at Twice-as-Nice Consignments passed our stringent *good-as-new* test. We sell only the finest quality clothing and home décor to meet the needs of the pickiest buyers." This new copy effectively catches the target audience's attention and appeals to their desire to save money (an emotional trigger). It also tells them exactly what they'll get by shopping at Twice-as-Nice Consignments. From reading this copy, the target audience knows they'll save money and get very high-quality items in good-as-new condition when they shop at Twice-as-Nice Consignments.

 REAL-WORLD EXAMPLES

McDonald's provides a helpful example of copywriting that tells customers what's in it for them with their campaign that said, "You deserve a break today." This copy successfully appealed to customers' on an emotional level and told them specifically what they would get by eating at McDonald's—a break from cooking, cleaning, and possibly even more depending on each customer's lifestyle. It's simple copy, but it made customers stop and think, "Hey, I *do* deserve a break."

Similarly, the U.S. Army used copy that said, "Be all that you can be" for a long time. With some products and services, it can be difficult to tell customers what's in it for them when they buy or try a product or service. The Army is certainly an organization that struggles with increasing their

CASE STUDY ABC TAX SERVICES

See Chapter 17 for the complete Copywriting Outline for ABC Tax Services as well as ad and marketing collateral samples using copy culled from the Copywriting Outline.

Copywriting Outline Step 4

Step 4: W.I.I.F.M. (What's In It For Me?)—How can I elaborate on my product's benefits and differentiators to tell customers how the product will positively affect their lives?

- Get money in your pocket *fast* with e-filing.
- You can put *more* money in your wallet because ABC Tax Services finds even the smallest deductions.
- Save money with *free* e-filing.
- Reduce the stress of tax time. Let the professionals at ABC Tax Services do the work for you.
- Never worry about an audit again. ABC Tax Services' audit protection service will help you if the IRS flags your return for audit.

recruitment numbers. By creating copy that appealed to their audience's desire to be given the opportunity to live up to their own potential (an effective emotional trigger), the Army boosted the amount of new recruits.

Recently, I saw a great example of "What's in it for me?" copywriting in a print ad for Cymbalta, a medication that treats depression. The copy in the ad read, "Depression hurts emotionally and physically. But you don't have to." The copy tells customers what they'll get if they use Cymbalta—relief. It's a well-crafted, clear, and concise message.

 ## SUMMARY

Effective copywriting needs to *specifically* describe how the product or service will *directly* affect the target audience's lives. Take the time to go through your Copywriting Outline and write a sentence or phrase for each feature, benefit, and differentiator that tells your target audience exactly how that feature, benefit, or differentiator will impact their lives. Do this for each of your target audiences if your product or business has more than one. Ask yourself the question, "What's in it for me?", as if you were a customer considering your product. What would you want to hear about the product before you decide to buy it? Those are the same questions your customers want answered.

If you have trouble separating yourself enough from your product or service to determine what customers are looking for, ask friends or family members for their opinions. One of the hardest things people can do is separate themselves from their work, so don't be afraid to ask for help from other people who can give you an unbiased view of the information customers need to know about what your product can do for them. Don't be surprised or offended if other people don't agree with your view. In fact, it's highly likely that they will provide very different opinions from your own. I'll discuss this in further detail in Chapter 9 where you'll learn how the features you think are important and are the most proud of might be very different from what your customers think are important.

chapter seven

step five
Focus on "You," Not "We"

REDUCE THE FLUFF

A critical component of copywriting is understanding the importance of each word you choose to use in an advertisement or marketing piece. Budget restraints, especially for small business owners, will force you to ensure that each word in your ad is there for a reason and truly adds value to your message. Advertising space and production methods are expensive, which often prohibits small to medium-size business owners from creating full-page ads or full-color brochures. Smaller ads mean less real estate to communicate your message. When that is the case, every word plays an extremely important role.

Analyze your copy word by word to ensure that each word is included for a reason and delete extraneous words that don't add value to your message. In fact, this is a practice copywriters should employ regardless of the budget, size of the ad, or marketing piece they are writing. Extra words can confuse or

LEARNING OBJECTIVES

How to write concise copy

▪

How to personalize
your copy

▪

How to apply the 80/20
rule to your copy

▪

How to make your copy
interactive and personal

▪

How to avoid corporate
rhetoric and jargon

slow down customers. Don't take the chance of losing a customer's interest with "fluff" words. Make sure your message is clear, concise, and direct by omitting filler words. This concept will be discussed in further detail in Chapter 9.

PRONOUNS—LITTLE WORDS WITH A BIG IMPACT ON COPYWRITING

It is essential that you are aware of how you're addressing your customers in your copy. To do this, you need to understand pronoun usage. Think back to your school days. Remember your English teacher explaining first person, second person, and third person? As a refresher, *first person* (I, me, my, mine, we, us, our, ours) is the person speaking and *second person* (you, your, yours) is the person to whom one is speaking. It's essential that you write copy that speaks *to* your target audience and not *at* them—and not about you. Therefore, the majority of your copy in any ad or marketing piece should be written in the second person. For example, do you prefer copy that says, "Through our first-rate sales department, we can deliver cars within 24-hours" or "You can drive your new car tomorrow"? While the first copy example focuses on the business, the second example focuses on customers and speaks directly to them. It's more personal, and thus, more effective.

Your copy should speak more about your customers and less about you.

Remember, writing in the second person helps your audience quickly connect the points in your copy to their own lives and allows them to personalize the advertisement or marketing piece. This is how the ad is connected to an individual customer's own life. By writing your copy so it focuses on the customer rather than yourself, the customer can personalize the ad and product you're selling and act accordingly.

APPLYING THE 80/20 RULE TO "YOU," NOT "WE"

The 80/20 rule introduced in Chapter 4 applies not only to Step 3 of the Copywriting Outline (Know Your Audience) but also to how you speak to your audience by using "you" more frequently than "we." As you have previously learned, when you're writing copy for an ad or marketing piece, focus on structuring your headlines and sentences so they are written primarily in the second person, thereby speaking directly to your customers. When you've completed writing the copy for your ad, take the time to read it and count how many times you used "you" (or another second person pronoun) vs. "we" (or another first person pronoun). As a rule of thumb, make sure you use second person pronouns in at least 80% of your copy and first person pronouns in no more than 20% of your copy. This will give you a good balance and ensure that your ad speaks directly to your customers.

To further understand the you vs. we concept, put yourself in your customers' shoes. How do you feel when you're talking to someone and the conversation is dominated by the other person speaking only about himself or herself? After a short amount of time, you probably don't pay much attention to what the other person is saying. However, if the conversation is more balanced or more about you, you probably pay much more attention and are actively involved in the discussion. The same concept holds true in copywriting and advertising. If an ad speaks only about the business in the first person, it's not as compelling to customers as an ad that speaks *about* and *to* those customers in the second person.

MAKE YOUR COPY INTERACTIVE AND CONVERSATIONAL

Again, similar to a verbal conversation, people don't pay as much attention if the other person is doing all the talking. When you write copy, you need to invite your customers to participate in the conversation (i.e., your ad or marketing piece). In fact, unless you're selling a highly technical or medical product, your copy should have a conversational tone, so customers are engaged and comfortable participating in the discussion. In other words, they'll be compelled to read the ad instead of ignoring it.

You can take the conversational tone a step further by adding questions and making your copy interactive. While it's important not to clutter your ad with questions (remember, you have limited real estate and need to use your ad space to get your key message, benefits, and differentiators across), one or two questions can make your ad interactive and invite your customers to join the conversation. Questions asked in the second person can help customers feel like they are being asked directly for their responses. For example, copy for a home alarm system ad could say, "Home invasions are on the rise. Is your family safe?" Not only does this copy focus on the emotional trigger of security, but it also uses the second person and asks a question making it interactive and more compelling for customers to read and act. While some questions can seem a bit cliché, they do have their place in copywriting when they are used strategically and effectively connect an ad to customers' individual lives.

Speak with your customers, not at them.

CORPORATE RHETORIC, JARGON, AND BUZZ WORDS IMPRESS YOUR COWORKERS—NOT YOUR CUSTOMERS

Consider these two copywriting examples for a photographer's business:

1. Paul's Wedding Photography operates under a unique business model that leverages technology to transfuse progressive X123-based digital imagery into the creation of best-in-class photographic results.
2. Paul's Wedding Photography uses the latest digital technology so your wedding day pictures look stunning for a lifetime of treasured memories.

The first example is teeming with jargon and buzz words and does little more than deliver an industry message that only another photographer would understand. On the other hand, the second example speaks directly to the customer and tells them that the photographer won't show up on the customer's wedding day with a Polaroid camera from 1985. Instead, the copy tells the customer that the photographer knows how to use current technology to provide great pictures. Your customer doesn't need to hear how many buzz words you know. They want to know what you and your product or service can do for them. Your copy needs to speak to your customers in terms to which they can relate.

A WORD ABOUT BUSINESS-TO-BUSINESS COPYWRITING

The majority of examples used in this book provide copywriting tips for ads and marketing pieces targeted to end-user consumer audiences (called business-to-consumer or B-to-C marketing). It's important to note that the basic copywriting rules apply whether you are writing messages for end-user customers, business partners, or business clients (called business-to-business or B-to-B marketing). However, your tone should be more professional in business-to-business copy, and the use of business jargon and buzz words is more acceptable. Always keep your target audience in mind as you craft your marketing messages and write copy in an appropriate tone and style for that audience.

Leave buzz words and jargon at the office.

EXAMPLES OF *"YOU," NOT "WE"* COPYWRITING

Use the following examples to help you change your copy from the first person to the second person, so it speaks directly to your customers rather than about you.

Product: Creative Craft Store—craft merchandise
Feature: low prices
Benefit: customers save money

Creative Craft Store wants to advertise their low prices. They could do this with copy that simply says, "We have the best prices." However, this copy focuses on the first person and doesn't speak to customers. By changing the copy to the second person, "You'll save money with Creative Craft Store's rock-bottom prices," the ad speaks directly to customers and helps them connect to their own lives a specific feature and benefit of visiting XYZ Craft Store.

By using "you" instead of "we," your copy focuses on the customer. In the previous example, the copy written in the second person allows customers to immediately connect the product or service to their own lives, making it more compelling. The copy written in the first person touts the company's claims but does not link it to customers personally. It is certainly nice that the company has the best prices, but potential customers might not understand what that means to them. The copywriter is responsible for communicating sales points in a way that the audience can relate to them. By telling customers they will save money with the company's low prices, they can personalize the advertisement and product, and they are more likely to be influenced by it.

Product: Microwave-Safe Containers
Feature: microwavable
Benefit: no burned fingers

Imagine a small business owner who sells kitchen products. She wants to place an ad that hypes her Microwave-Safe Containers to her target audience of mothers with small children. She could use copy that says, "Our Microwave-Safe Containers are made from our specially manufactured materials that don't get hot." This copy does not speak to customers and does not invite them to read more. However, if the copy is changed to say, "Are you tired of burning your fingers on scorching hot bowls from the microwave? Put your potholders away because Microwave-Safe Containers are cool to the touch straight from the microwave." The new copy asks customers a question, making it interactive and conversational, and it speaks directly to them in the second person, which motivates them to read more.

Product: Monique Jackson's Realtor Services
Feature: flexible schedule
Benefit: available to help customers anytime

Assume Monique Jackson is a realtor who focuses on service to win new customers. One of the best features of her service is her flexible schedule. She could write copy that says, "Monique Jackson is available anytime." This copy states exactly what Monique offers through her service, but it doesn't speak to the customer. If Monique changed her copy to say, "Do you want to tour a house on the market *right now*? No problem. Monique Jackson is available to help you day or night." Now the copy is interactive and very conversational. By using the second person, her message speaks directly to customers and allows them to personalize and relate to the copy.

 ## REAL-WORLD EXAMPLES

Recently, I was looking at theme park ticket prices for Walt Disney World. I noticed the copy Disney uses for their various park tickets is a great example of "you," not "we" copywriting. Disney uses the tagline, "Disney's Magic Y*our* Way," whenever they advertise their park tickets. Disney even goes so far as making the tagline into a logo that appears on all of their park ticket marketing literature and advertisements. Their tagline tells customers they can enjoy the magic of Disney their own way if they use the flexible ticketing options. This copy does a great job of tying together the product and Disney's entire brand image in a way that directly appeals to the customer.

A famous example of copy that successfully uses "you" rather than "we" is the Burger King campaign that says, "Have it your way." It's so simple, yet so effective. This campaign launched during a time when it was unheard of to alter a menu item at a fast food restaurant. Burger King appealed to their audience's desire to have fast food just the way they wanted it. No tomatoes? No problem. To this day, Burger King lets their customers make choices and feel satisfied and special. The copy successfully hypes these benefits and appeals to emotional triggers.

Similarly, Hallmark ran the, "When you care enough to send the very best" campaign for many years. This copy was clever in several ways. Not only did it speak directly to the audience by using "you," but it also appealed to the audience's emotional triggers. Suddenly, buying a greeting card was equivalent to buying jewelry. "Do you care enough to buy a diamond or just cubic zirconia?" translated into "Do you care enough to buy Hallmark or just some other greeting card brand?" Furthermore, Hallmark successfully differentiated themselves from their competition by making customers think their cards were "the very best." It's amazing how one sentence of well-written copy can say so much.

SUMMARY

Remember to write copy that speaks *to* your customers not *at* them by using the second person significantly more than the first person. This is a simple way to link your product's features directly to your customers' lives. Make sure your customers can relate to your copy by using a conversational tone and invite them to join the conversation with questions, but remember to adjust your tone to correspond to the target audience for each ad or marketing piece you create. Review the benefits and differentiators you developed in Steps 1 and 2 of the Copywriting Outline and rewrite them to include the second person. This way, when the time comes to write your ads, you will have completed most of your work already. You will be able to simply pick and choose the phrases you need from your Copywriting Outline for each ad based on your target audience and the medium where you're placing your ad. I'll discuss this further in Step 6 of the Copywriting Outline.

CASE STUDY ABC TAX SERVICES

See Chapter 17 for the complete Copywriting Outline for ABC Tax Services as well as ad and marketing collateral samples using copy culled from the Copywriting Outline.

Copywriting Outline Step 5

Step 5: "You," Not "We"—How can I word my product's benefits and differentiators so they talk *to* the customer and not *about* me?

- What do you want to spend your tax refund on this year? Pay down some bills? Go on vacation? Whatever you want to do with that money, you can do it faster with ABC Tax Services' free e-filing program.

- You've already waited long enough for your tax refund. Don't wait any longer.

- Tax time stressing you out? You deserve some peace of mind. Call ABC Tax Services and forget about those worries.

chapter eight

step six
Understand Your Medium

UNDERSTANDING THE VARIOUS FORMS OF MARKETING AND ADVERTISING MEDIA

As you write your copy, be aware that each different medium where an ad is placed requires a different tone or style. Depending on where you're placing your ad, the copy you use changes based on the audience who will see the ad. Are you placing your ad in a local newspaper or on a billboard? Are you placing your ad in a woman's magazine or in a news magazine? Different media require different copy to most effectively persuade a particular audience to act. Furthermore, different types of marketing pieces require different types of copy. Remember, there are many ways to use copy to promote your business other than traditional advertisements. Use every possible and appropriate opportunity to communicate your marketing messages to your customers. Chapter 13 provides a detailed explanation of some of the most common forms of

LEARNING OBJECTIVES

The different forms of advertising and marketing

▪

How to match your copy to your ad's placement or the purpose of your marketing piece

▪

The relationship between design and copy

marketing and advertising media. Following is a brief list of popular marketing and advertising opportunities:

- Print ads (magazines, newspapers, newsletters, telephone books, etc.)
- Television ads
- Radio ads
- Outdoor ads (billboards, signage, ads on vehicles, etc.)
- Online ads (banner ads, text ads, sponsored reviews, etc.)
- Websites
- Blogs
- Brochures
- Point-of-sale signage and displays (banners, posters, window decals, counter cards, tent cards, etc.)
- Direct mail or email
- Newsletters
- Press releases
- Speeches or sales presentations
- Flyers
- Coupons
- Stationery (business cards, letterhead, envelopes, folders, invoices, etc.)
- Billing inserts

MATCHING YOUR COPY TO YOUR MEDIUM

An essential part of creating advertising and using your budget wisely is to select the most appropriate form and placement for your ad or marketing piece. Now is the time to put to work the demographic profile you created in Step 3 of the Copywriting Outline. Use your demographic profile information to select the most appropriate medium for your target audience, then choose the best location

Use every opportunity to communicate your marketing messages to consumers.

within that medium that will have the broadest audience appeal. This is the best place to invest your advertising dollars and get the biggest response. For example, the owner of a bookstore might choose to advertise in a print publication because she knows her target audience is made up of avid readers. She now needs to select a location in the appropriate print publication that will ensure her audience sees the ad. Selecting the television guide section of a local newspaper is probably not the best choice if the bookstore owner wants to find avid readers and generate the highest response from the advertisement. Instead, the local or national new sections and the editorial section might be better choices based on the demographic profile of the target audience.

Messages can be consistent across various media, but the copy you write should change to match each medium.

Let's consider another example. A barbershop owner will undoubtedly get a better return on his advertising investment if he places an ad in the sports section of the local newspaper rather than a flyer at the grocery store. He knows that his target audience of men is more likely to read the sports section then go grocery shopping. Of course, this is a generalization, but without a large budget to conduct wide-scale demographic research, you'll have to improvise and make some assumptions related to your target customers' behaviors to try to get the biggest bang for your buck in terms of ad placement.

Once you've selected the best medium to place your ad, you'll need to adjust your copy to fit that medium. Fortunately, you already completed Step 1 through Step 5 of the Copywriting Outline and created a variety of personalized sentences and phrases related to your product's benefits and differentiators. Now you simply need to tweak the copy you've already written to match your medium. Usually, you'll need to adjust your copy to the amount of space available in your medium. For example, a full-page ad in your local telephone book includes significantly more copy than a quarter-page ad. Alternatively, a radio ad includes very different verbiage than a billboard ad.

To further explain this concept, consider that a billboard ad has just seconds to communicate a message to a person traveling in a vehicle at 65 mph. Alternatively, a radio advertisement needs to quickly grab the listener's attention to ensure that he or she doesn't change the station. However, a radio ad has an opportunity to convey additional information once the listener's attention is captured. A billboard ad does not have that additional opportunity. Therefore, the copy used in radio advertising is very different from the copy used in billboard advertising. Each medium has its own set of requirements, restrictions, challenges, and opportunities for you to consider as you create your copy.

UNDERSTANDING THE RELATIONSHIP BETWEEN COPY AND DESIGN

At its core, copywriting is the tool you use to communicate your marketing messages and drive business results. The design of your ads and marketing collateral should enhance that message. The purpose of design is to assist in capturing the attention of your audience and guide them through your ad, so they see the entire message you're trying to communicate. Design is meant to help make the most important elements of your message stand out from the supporting information, and it's an essential part of advertising and marketing. However, I believe that copywriting should stand on its own without design. Your message is the most important element in your ad. Don't give up any of your message to make room for a great design. While a design tends to have a short lifespan, a message can live for a long time through word-of-mouth marketing, online social media marketing, and more.

Work with your designer to develop a creative design that enhances your message and makes it more powerful and effective. I admit that over the years there have been many immensely popular ads that have relied heavily on concept or design, but these examples do not make up the majority of the best and most compelling ads and marketing pieces. Don't fall victim to an innovative design unless it helps communicate your message. Remember, your message—not your design—should lead your marketing effort. The relationship between design and copy will be discussed further in Chapter 14.

RESEARCH YOUR COMPETITION

When you are selecting the appropriate medium and placement for your advertising or marketing, it is very useful to research your competitors' ads and marketing pieces. This will help you make the best, strategic decisions. It's critical to familiarize yourself with the different mediums your competitors use and study the ads that you think work well within those mediums. Use the ads that work the best as a guide to help you develop your own ad. If an ad that only uses one or two lines of copy seems more compelling to you than an ad with one or two paragraphs, then create your ad in a similar fashion. The ads that capture your attention will most likely capture the attention of your audience, too. Make sure the information you include in those one or two lines of copy are the most compelling for your target audience and will drive them to action thereby boosting your sales.

EXAMPLES OF *UNDERSTAND YOUR MEDIUM* COPYWRITING

As you've learned, each type of medium requires different copy to effectively communicate your message and drive business. The following examples will help you see how copy can be adjusted for optimum effectiveness in various media.

Product: City Salon—haircuts and styling
Feature: low price
Benefit: save money

In this example, City Salon plans to focus their marketing plan on attracting new customers. To reach this goal, they want to appeal to the emotional trigger of potential customers' desire to save money. The salon plans to advertise their low prices on a banner they will hang outside their salon as well as in a brochure they will hand out or mail to prospective clients. The real estate on a banner is very limited, so the best copywriting approach is to be very direct by communicating the most important benefits that will drive customers to act. Effective signage copy could say, "50% off professional haircuts." The copy is short and to the point and catches the attention of customers' by pushing one of their emotional triggers (the desire to save money). The City Salon's brochure could include more detailed copy because the medium provides more space in which to work. For example, the same low price feature could be communicated using copy that says, "Save 50% on your next haircut. At City Salon, you'll receive a professional haircut from one of our highly trained and experienced stylists for just $9.95." Because the brochure has more copy real estate, City Salon can elaborate on the benefits of their low price. The same message is communicated in both the banner and brochure, but the copy changed to complement each medium.

Product: Abdul's Handyman Services—home repairs
Feature: quality service
Benefit: peace-of-mind that the job is done right

Abdul's Handyman Services wants to send a direct mail piece to families in his neighborhood. Using direct mail, Abdul has enough space to include copy that not only mentions the key feature and differentiator of his business (quality service), but also the benefits of that feature and choosing his business. For example, his direct mail copy could say, "Stop worrying. Whether you need a cracked tile replaced, a fence repaired, or a garage door installed, Abdul's Handyman Services will do it right the first time." In a direct mail piece, Abdul can include more copy about the features and benefits of his business. However, if he places a business card size ad in his neighborhood's homeowners' association newsletter, he will have significantly less space, and his copy will need to be shorter and to the point. He could say, "If you want the job done right the first time, call Abdul's Handyman Services." This copy has the same message as the direct mail piece, but leaves out some benefit details that are too text heavy for such a small ad space.

Product: Tiny Tots Daycare—childcare
Feature: security
Benefit: children are safe, less worry for parents

Assume that Tiny Tots Daycare determines from their demographic research (most likely through talking with existing customers) that mothers are typically the ultimate decision makers when it comes to selecting a daycare center for their children and that security is a key benefit and emotional trigger for current and prospective customers. Tiny Tots Daycare also learns that most of the mothers in their target audience watch the local television station, so they decide to film a commercial and air it on that station. Copy in a television ad is very different from print copy because television is a more visual medium. For example, Tiny Tots Daycare wants to focus on their internet security cameras to appeal to customers' desire for a safe and secure daycare center. With that in mind, Tiny Tots Daycare could film a television commercial that *shows* their internet security cameras and how those cameras allow parents to see their children throughout the day. Tiny Tots could also highlight their alarms in a commercial (visually and audibly) as another way to communicate their security features. The script that accompanies the commercial could say, "Our security features keep every child at Tiny Tots Daycare safe at all times." The copy doesn't need to elaborate on the specific security features because the viewers will *see* them on their TV screens.

However, if Tiny Tots Daycare decides to create a brochure to distribute to prospective customers, the copy needs to be very detailed and explain the features and benefits of Tiny Tots Daycare's security systems. Effective brochure copy could say, "You can rest assured that your children are safe at Tiny Tots Daycare. Not only are your children secured by a sophisticated alarm system on all doors, but you can also watch your little ones throughout the day on your computer by accessing our online video cameras through our website. You'll always know what your children are doing, and you'll have peace of mind that they're as safe as if they were right by your side." This copy is much more detailed and specifically tells customers the safety features that are in place at Tiny Tots Daycare and how the features will benefit them. In fact, an effective way to communicate these features and benefits is a bulleted list that calls attention to them. Unlike the television commercial, where customers can see the security features at work, the brochure needs to give more details so customers can understand how these features will directly impact their lives.

 ## REAL-WORLD EXAMPLES

Creating copy that effectively works in the medium in which you're placing your ad can also affect your ad concept. For example, the famous Federal Express TV ads that featured the Fast Talker would not be as effective in print. Additionally, ads that rely heavily on visuals work well with less copy. For example, I recently saw an ad for Scott Extra Soft Toilet Tissue in a magazine. The only copy included in the ad was, "Our softest ever." The photo in the ad showed a man blowing bubbles at a package and the bubbles not breaking. They simply bounced off the soft toilet tissue. This small amount of copy would not work in a radio campaign because it relies so heavily on the photo. The copy in a radio ad needs to be more detailed and clearly explain the benefits and features of Scott Extra Soft Toilet Tissue.

Similarly, I saw a billboard by Cadillac advertising their Escalade sport utility vehicle. The billboard featured a photograph of an Escalade, the Cadillac logo, and copy that merely said, "The new Escalade." This is a perfect example of simple copy that works well on a billboard, but would fail in other mediums. For example, a television or radio commercial about the vehicle would be more effective if it offered additional details that hype the superior features of the new Escalade. The details appeal to the emotional

CASE STUDY ABC TAX SERVICES

See Chapter 17 for the complete Copywriting Outline for ABC Tax Services as well as ad and marketing collateral samples using copy culled from the Copywriting Outline.

Copywriting Outline Step 6

Step 6: Know Your Medium—Where will I be advertising? How can I write copy to maximize the space provided by the medium?

- Placing an ad in the local newspaper's lifestyles section where the target audience is likely to see it. Benefits to focus on:
  - Fast refund
  - Maximum refund
  - Free e-filing

triggers of wanting to be a leader or keeping up with the Joneses, thereby creating a perceived need for a high-end car like a Cadillac Escalade.

Alternatively, your promotion and corresponding message might need to change based on your medium. For example, email campaigns that use free shipping promotions are very effective in driving consumers to make online purchases. Recently, I received an email from Pottery Barn Kids with a subject line that read, "Free shipping on summer baby clothing." This is a great online offer with straightforward, effective copy. However, the offer and copy would not be as effective in a store promotional flyer or Sunday newspaper circular where the audience is typically looking for in-store sales and discounts.

SUMMARY

Remember, copywriting is significantly impacted by the medium where you choose to place your ad. There are differences not only between the amount of real estate available in different mediums, but also in the amount of visual support each medium provides. While copy for signage or radio advertisements must be short, succinct, and direct, copy for brochures or direct mail can be more verbose, subtle, and detailed. Media that provide enough space to include extensive details in your copy can be the most challenging to write because you run the risk of saying too much. The next step in the Copywriting Outline will teach you how to avoid including too much information in your advertisement or marketing piece.

chapter nine

step seven
Avoid T.M.I.
(Too Much Information)

GET TO THE POINT

Never risk losing the attention of your audience by providing too much detail in your copy. Effective copywriting tells your audience what they need to know to act and make a purchase or how to contact you for more information. Extraneous details clutter the minds of your audience, which increases the possibility of them forgetting the most important aspects of your advertisement or marketing program. Unless you're advertising a prescription drug, highly technical equipment, or an exceedingly regulated or complicated product, the best rule to follow is K.I.S.S. (Keep It Simple Stupid). You're spending a substantial amount of your advertising budget on placing each ad. With each ad, you only receive a small amount of space to get your message across to your audience. Wisely use that pricey real estate to ensure you get the highest return on your investment.

LEARNING OBJECTIVES

How to remove filler words from your copy

▪

The K.I.S.S. and T.M.I. rules

▪

How to trim extraneous information from your copy

▪

How to tweak your copy to fit your design

▪

How to resist using big words and jargon in your copy

The best way to determine the most important aspect of the message for your target audience is to work backward by pretending you are one of your most valuable customers. At this point, you have completed the first six steps of the Copywriting Outline, so you already should know what features, benefits, differentiators, and emotional triggers are most likely to have the biggest impact on your target customers' individual lives, and you also know how to write personalized copy touting these benefits and differentiators while tying them directly to your customers. Now you simply need to select the key sentences and phrases that will appeal to your customers based on the amount of space your ad provides.

Too much information clutters the most important messages.

One of the biggest pitfalls in advertising occurs when an ad or marketing piece provides a significant amount of space. It's tempting for the novice copywriter to fill that space with every fact and detail related to the product or service being sold. While you want to make sure your target audience hears your entire story, you'll lose their attention if your story is too long. Similarly, if you're having a conversation with someone and the story they are telling is too long, your mind wanders, and ultimately, you don't hear it entirely. The same holds true when reading or listening to ad copy. If there is too much information to absorb, customers lose interest.

SHOW NO MERCY FOR FILLER WORDS

In addition to focusing on communicating the most important information in your copy, you also need to avoid cluttering your ad with too many words. Once you complete your copywriting project, review it with a critical eye. Are there any points that can be rewritten for clarity? Can extraneous words be deleted? In fact, deleting extra words is one of the best ways to make your copy tighter and more compelling. Avoid filler words like *really* and *that*. Be cautious of overusing adverbs and adjectives, which are notorious for cluttering otherwise good copy. For example, copy for a local plumber's ad could say, "ABC Plumbing is

CLOSEUP

The K.I.S.S. Rule of Copywriting
Keep It Simple Stupid

very experienced and really understands your needs." In this example, the words "very" and "really" do not add value to the copy at all. Instead, they simply clutter the copy with extra words. By eliminating these extraneous words, the copy follows the K.I.S.S. rule and becomes easier to read and more compelling, "ABC Plumbing is experienced and understands your needs."

BIG WORDS CAN BE CONFUSING AND UNIMPRESSIVE

One of the most important things to keep in mind is that you're writing copy for an audience who has very little time to spend looking at your advertisement or marketing piece. This rule is not just about the content of your message, but also the specific words you use to communicate that message. The best rule of thumb to follow ties directly into the K.I.S.S. rule: keep your message and words simple. Don't try to impress your audience with your ability to use the thesaurus. Instead, impress them with benefits.

Furthermore, don't use what marketers like to call $10 words when a $1 word will do. For example, don't tell your customers your vegetable chopper helps them cut vegetables "expeditiously." Instead, tell them it cuts vegetables "fast." Not only do big words slow down readers, but they also come across as arrogant or even boring. You're not trying to sell your writing skills; you're trying to sell a product or service. Don't forget this objective when you're creating copy. Your copy should

> *Don't feel like you have to fill all the space provided in an ad. White space is your friend.*

match the expectations of your audience. If you're writing copy for busy mothers, use words to which they respond. Alternatively, if you're writing copy for scientists, use language that audience understands and appreciates.

Remember, copywriting is not just one style of writing. Rather it's an amalgamation of various methods and tactics used to speak directly to a wide array of audiences. With each copywriting project, you'll wear a slightly different hat depending on the goals of that marketing initiative. Your role as the copywriter is to meet the objectives of that program through effective communications.

Don't try to impress your audience with big words or jargon. Simple messages are easier to understand, remember, and act upon.

LEAVE JARGON IN THE OFFICE

While you might be able to impress your friends and colleagues with your ability to embrace the latest jargon and buzz words, customers are far less influenced by these words. In fact, many customers are completely turned off by copy that is wrought with jargon and buzz words. Of course, there are some audiences who do respond positively to copy that includes jargon (for example, the target audience for a business-to-business ad), and you'll need to make that determination when you identify the target audience for your ad or marketing piece. However, the majority of consumers respond to simple language more quickly than copy heavy in jargon and buzz words.

For example, consider an ad from a local computer store promoting their technical assistance program. The company could use copy that says, "Our business operates under a unique paradigm leveraging ABC-X solutions." Most consumers would respond saying, "What?" The company doesn't sound knowledgeable or capable. Instead, they sound confusing and offer no useful information. The copy is meaningless to consumers. If the copy was revised to say, "An expert technician will get your computer working fast," it has more personal meaning to customers.

✹ CLOSEUP

Examples of Jargon to Use Cautiously in Copywriting

- Benchmark
- Best in class
- Best practices
- Continuum
- Grassroots
- Infrastructure
- Leverage
- Methodology
- Metrics
- Objective
- Organic
- Output
- Paradigm
- Selling proposition
- Strategy
- Synergy
- Tactic
- Target
- Value added
- Value proposition

To which of these ads would you respond? I would call the company in the second example. Not only does the copy tell consumers the company employs experts, but they also respond quickly. The customer doesn't need to know the extraneous information included in the first copy example; they just need to know someone will get the job done.

THE BENEFITS OF BEING SHORT AND SWEET

Have you ever been in a conversation with someone and it seems to take that person forever to get to the point of his or her story? Have you listened intently but thought, "Hurry up"? An important rule to remember in copywriting is to never let your audience feel that way. Instead, you want to quickly hook them with an effective headline and then tease them with a useful subhead. Finally, you want to drive home your key selling points and create a sense of urgency that motivates your audience to act. Copywriting should never be passive. It must always be action-oriented, concise, to the point, and clear. There is no room for confusion. Boring your audience with extraneous information that doesn't affect their purchasing decision only clutters your message.

Naturally, there are many aspects of your business that you are particularly proud of and want the world to know. However, each ad or marketing piece has a specific goal attached to it that must be identified up-front. Your copy needs to help you reach that goal. If a piece of copy is counter effective to reaching that goal, delete it. I call this the T.M.I. (Too Much Information) rule, and I equate the practice to cleaning out a closet. Professional home organizers tell their customers to show no mercy when cleaning clutter. Their rule states that if you haven't used an item in a year, it's garbage. Copywriting works the same way. If a word or phrase doesn't support your overall message and goal for your marketing piece, it's garbage. That doesn't mean that a particular word or phrase of copy is useless. Remember the old saying, one man's trash is another man's treasure. This holds true for copywriting, too. The copy you don't use today could be just the right message for a future marketing campaign. Record the unused copy in your Copywriting Outline in

Don't bore your audience. Get to the point!

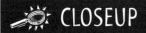

The T.M.I. Rule of Copywriting
Avoid Too Much Information

case an opportunity arises in the future when those words might help you effectively communicate your message. Remember, your Copywriting Outline is a working document. You should constantly update and revise it to help you write copy for future marketing campaigns. What you write or what you delete from your current copywriting project might be useful for a future project.

THE RED PEN RULE

A tool I like to use to ensure my copy is succinct and, therefore, powerful is what I call the Red Pen Rule. Once you have written your final copy and feel it's compelling and tight, get your red pen and delete at least 30% of it. Chances are that 30% does not truly help drive your message, and your copy will be better off without it. Of course, 30% is not a hard and fast rule. The idea is to delete more than just a few words. For the Red Pen Rule to work and actually make your copy more effective, you need to delete a significant amount of text. If you're doubtful, test the Red Pen Rule by asking the opinions of friends, family, and colleagues. Show them the longer and shorter versions of your copy or actually run each version of your ad and then analyze the results.

TWEAKING COPY TO FIT THE DESIGN OF YOUR MARKETING PIECE

The T.M.I. rule tells copywriters to avoid providing too much information, and it goes hand-in-hand with the design and layout of your ad or marketing piece. Often, you won't recognize that your copy is too long for your ad space until your designer lays out the text and graphic elements. Trimming copy can be a painful and continual process. An essential rule copywriters must follow is to never get too attached to your copy. Most importantly, don't think that the copy you deliver to a designer is final. More often than not, after the design process has begun you'll need to edit your copy to fit it in your ad space in a visually appealing manner. Design is a critical component of catching your target audience's attention and enhancing your marketing message, so you may have to sacrifice less powerful copy elements or add copy that works with the design you choose thereby creating the most compelling ad overall.

LOOKING THROUGH YOUR CUSTOMERS' EYES

Throughout this book, I have mentioned the importance of looking at your advertising and marketing efforts, including your copywriting, through the eyes of your customers. It's essential to take a step back from your product or service and see it exactly how your customers do. This will enable you to determine the most compelling features, benefits, and differentiators from their points of view. By focusing on your *customers'* wants and needs rather than on the features and benefits that *you* like, you'll improve your copy, drive your customers to action, and boost your profits significantly.

EXAMPLES OF *T.M.I.* COPYWRITING

Following are examples of several ways you can trim copy to make it more compelling.

Product: SOS Home Security—residential alarm systems
Feature: fifty customer service representatives
Benefit: easy to talk to someone to fix problems or place orders

Let's imagine that SOS Home Security wants to hype the fact that they employ 50 customer service representatives. They're proud of this number, which is significantly higher than the number of customer service representatives their competitors employ. SOS Home Security could hype this feature in their copy by saying, "We have over 50 customer service representatives in our call center." However, this example demonstrates copywriting that focuses on an extraneous detail customers do not need to know. While SOS Home Security is proud of having a staff of 50 customer service representatives, it is probably not the most important piece of information to tell customers to compel them to act and buy a home security system. In fact, when customers hear this information they are more likely to say, "Who cares that SOS Home Security has 50 customer sales representatives?"

More importantly, customers want to know if they have any problems after buying a home security system, it will be easy to get help. With this in mind, the copy could be rewritten to say, "When you need help, just call SOS Home Security's customer service line. Your call will be answered fast and by a live person every time." This copy omits the extraneous detail included in the original example. The fact that SOS Home Security employs 50 customer service representatives is irrelevant to customers, but the fact that *because* SOS Home Security employs 50 customer service representatives a live person will always be available to help when customers call, is likely to be an important contribution to their purchase decisions. Bottom-line, SOS Home Security may be proud of its 50 customer service representatives, but that extra information isn't important to customers. However, when the information is rewritten without the extraneous number, it becomes a compelling benefit to customers and an effective differentiator from the competition.

Product: Smith Power Washing—power washing services
Feature: clean all surfaces
Benefit: one-stop shopping

Smith Power Washing is a family-owned local business with the appropriate equipment, team, and experience to clean any surface. They want to promote their business as offering one-stop shopping for all types of pressure washing needs. They could advertise using copy that says, "We can clean your concrete, wood, pavers, driveway, porch, house, roof, deck, fence, patio, dock, or garage floor." This copy certainly tells customers what Smith Power Washing can do for them, but it provides too much information and doesn't compel the target audience to act. Unless an ad or brochure includes a specific section where a list of services can be used as a separate call out from the main copy for the ad, the copy is too detailed and too text heavy.

More compelling copy that succinctly tells the story of Smith Power Washing's extensive services could be, "Smith Power Washing can take care of all your power washing needs. Fence, house, deck, you name it; we'll make it look like new." The copy in the second example focuses on the benefits to customers rather than on Smith Power Washing's laundry list of services. By simply saying they can handle any cleaning job, they are able to delete the list of services and instead use the space to promote additional benefits and differentiators that customers can relate to personally and help drive their customers to action.

Product: Beachtown Jewelry Repair—jewelry repairs
Feature: local business for 20 years,
member of local chamber of commerce
Benefit: trustworthy

Beachtown Jewelry Repair wants customers to understand they can drop off their fine jewelry for repairs and not worry about their items being lost or stolen. The owner thinks the best way to communicate this trustworthiness is by letting customers know she has been in business for over twenty years and belongs to the local chamber of commerce. She creates copy that says, "Visit Beachtown Jewelry Repair—your local jeweler and proud member of the Beachtown Chamber of Commerce for 20 years." This copy certainly tells customers the features the owner thinks customers need to know to deem her trustworthy, but it doesn't offer much incentive for customers to visit the shop.

Many customers are not fazed by the overused claims of affiliations that local businesses tout in advertisements. Being a member of the local chamber of commerce does not motivate customers to choose Beachtown Jewelry Repair over any other jewelry store (some of which are probably also members of the local chamber of commerce). If the owner changes her copy to focus on her customers' needs and emotional triggers while eliminating extraneous information, she will create copy that is more action-oriented. For example, revised copy could say, "Beachtown Jewelry Repair has carefully and meticulously repaired Beachtown residents' personal treasures for the past 20 years. You can trust your finest jewelry to our expert, secure hands." The copy no longer mentions Beachtown Jewelry Repair's membership in the local chamber of commerce. Instead, it focuses on customers' needs for security and trust when they choose a jeweler to repair their expensive items.

 ## REAL-WORLD EXAMPLES

Verizon Wireless currently uses an ad campaign that demonstrates how to avoid too much information in copy. The company uses copy that simply says, "Can you hear me now? Audiences quickly learned that the answer is "yes." Verizon Wireless customers get reception just about everywhere, which is significantly better than the competition can claim. The ads usually provide more copy, but as long as customers walk away with the "Can you hear me now?" phrase in their heads, Verizon Wireless has successfully communicated their message.

Copy for Bounty paper towels ads once referred to Bounty as, "The quicker-picker-upper." Nothing else needed to be said. In fact, I can't even remember if those ads provided any other information. Customers simply walked away knowing that Bounty paper towels could pick up spills quicker

CASE STUDY ABC TAX SERVICES

See Chapter 17 for the complete Copywriting Outline for ABC Tax Services as well as ad and marketing collateral samples using copy culled from the Copywriting Outline.

Copywriting Outline Step 7

Step 7: Avoid T.M.I. (Too Much Information)—What information is important to me but not helpful in an ad (i.e., may be useful in a news article or brochure in the future)? How can I keep my ad copy from becoming cluttered?

- Examples of jargon to avoid:
  - Practitioner
- Elements that can be omitted from a newspaper ad to taxpayers expecting a refund (limited space for key messages):
  - Audit protection
  - Confidence Guarantee
  - Staffing

than any other paper towel. What else did they need to know? Nothing, and the ads reflected that by omitting extraneous copy.

Another example comes from Thomasville Furniture. The main copy in their recent television commercials states, "Thomasville. So you." This tagline not only personalizes the copy, but it also says a lot in a few words. There is no need to elaborate with an exhaustive list of the types of people who like Thomasville Furniture. The copy infers that anyone watching the commercial will like Thomasville's furniture. It's simple, yet effective.

SUMMARY

The most important part of successfully completing Step 7 of the Copywriting Outline requires you to look at your ad from a 10-foot view. That means you need to step back and look at it impartially. If you were a customer considering buying your product, what information would you need to see in an ad to motivate you to act and buy that product? Those are the critical aspects that need to be included in your copy.

Using the work you've done in Step 1 through Step 6 of the Copywriting Outline, choose the phrases and sentences that most effectively get your message across to your target audience and selected medium. Edit your copy. Then edit it again and again to ensure you've deleted filler words and extraneous details. What's left should be clear, concise copy that drives your target audience to action. In Step 8, you will tell them exactly what action to take.

chapter ten

step eight
Include a Call to Action

BE ACTIVE, NOT PASSIVE

The goal of any ad or marketing piece is to elicit some kind of response from the audience who sees it. A call to action is the element of copy that tells an audience how you want them to respond to your advertisement or marketing piece. Typically, the call to action creates a sense of urgency around a message and provides instructions on what to do next. For example, a call to action might tell the audience to call the advertiser or visit their store or website.

Including a call to action is by far the most important aspect of effective copywriting. It is essential that you make it easy for your audience to act on your ad or marketing message. You already persuaded them to want your product by following Step 1 through Step 7 of the Copywriting Outline and by writing influential copy. Now you must make sure your audience can respond easily to your ad and buy your product by compelling them to act.

LEARNING OBJECTIVES

The difference between active and passive voice sentence structure and how it affects your copy

■

How to add a sense of urgency to your copy

■

How to incorporate a response mechanism into your copy

■

Copy tips to aid in tracking the return on your advertising investment

To start, make sure the sentence structure of your copywriting is in an active rather than passive voice. The reason for this is simple. Copy that you write in the active voice is by definition action-oriented, while copy that you write in the passive voice talks about the action in a remote manner. To further explain, when you write a sentence in the active voice, the subject of the sentence *performs* the action of the verb in the sentence. On the other hand, if you write a sentence in the passive voice, the subject of the sentence *receives* the action from the verb of the sentence.

Your copy should drive customers to action now, not make them think about maybe acting later.

Following are some examples of advertising copy for Amy's Edibles that demonstrate the difference between active and passive voice:

- **Passive:** Your party will be catered by Amy's Edibles detail-oriented staff members.
- **Active:** Amy's Edibles caters your party to the finest detail.
- **Passive:** Berries have been hand picked for Amy's Edibles Jam to make sure customers have purchased the freshest and tastiest product.
- **Active:** We hand pick every berry for Amy's Edibles Jam, so it's the freshest and tastiest you can buy.

Both of these examples rephrase the passive sentences to make them active and more compelling. (See the Closeup Box for more examples of passive voice vs. active voice). An active sentence is motivational and more likely to compel your customers to act. Don't agonize over writing in the active voice while you're writing your copy. Instead, put together a draft of your copy and then go back and change the sentences written in the passive voice to the active voice. Look at each sentence and ask yourself, "Could I write this sentence in a clearer, more action-oriented way?" You don't need to change every sentence written in the passive voice to the active voice. You simply want to make sure your copy sounds clear, concise, and actionable.

🔍 CLOSEUP

Examples of Passive and Active Voice Sentence Structures

- **Passive:** The letter is being written by John.
- **Active:** John writes the letter.
- **Passive:** The movie will be released in June.
- **Active:** The studio will release the movie in June.
- **Passive:** This season of *American Idol* was watched by more than 50% of Americans.
- **Active:** More than 50% of Americans watched this season of *American Idol*.

CREATE A SENSE OF URGENCY

The second step in creating an effective call to action in your copy is developing a sense of urgency. Your goal in advertising is to create awareness of your product or service and, ultimately, boost sales. When do you want to do that? Do you want your customers to act tomorrow, next month, or next year? If you're spending money on advertising now, you most likely want your customers to act now. If that's the case, your copy needs to tell them to get off the couch and get into your store *now*. There are many words and phrases you can add to your copy to create a sense of urgency.

This is a good time to point out that you need to be careful about using exclamation points in your copy. When you write copy, it can be easy to fall into the trap of overusing exclamation points to emphasize your messages. One or two exclamation points can help drive the importance of a sentence home, but too many exclamation points clutter copy and mitigate their effectiveness. Save exclamation points for places where they'll have a strong impact—like creating a sense of urgency in your call to action.

Don't suggest action. Demand it.

CLOSEUP

Words and Phrases that Effectively Create a Sense of Urgency in Copywriting

- Act now
- Don't delay
- Hurry in
- Call today
- For a limited time only
- Don't miss it
- While supplies last
- Call now
- Available only to the first ## callers
- This weekend only
- Don't wait any longer
- One-time offer
- Get yours today

MAKE IT EASY FOR CUSTOMERS TO ACT

Don't forget to tell your audience how to find you through a website address, telephone number, email address, or street address. It seems simple, but the number of ads I see that don't tell customers how to easily contact the advertiser or purchase the product or service constantly amazes me. These days, with email becoming as popular as telephones, copy needs to include a phone number and email address at a minimum. For ads promoting a physical location, copy should include a street address, simple directions, or a landmark. Remember, these days many people are either too lazy or too busy to research a store location or phone number. Any information that makes it easier for your customers to find you and buy your product is important and should be included in your copy.

Preparing employees to assist customers who respond to your advertisement or marketing piece is just as important as the ad itself. Your employees must be knowledgeable about your ad or promotional offer before customers start contacting your business. For example, if you place an ad offering a buy one, get one free discount and a customer calls to inquire about the promotion, you don't want your employee to say, "I don't know anything about that deal." The prospective customer will hang up and will be unlikely to choose your business in the future. Instead, train your employees and anyone else who interacts with existing and potential customers. Your business needs to present a consistent message from your advertising to your customer relations and all points in between. You can read more about consistency in communications and branding in Chapter 14.

People are busy. Don't make them do more work than they have to. Make it easy for them to follow your instructions to act.

TRACK YOUR RESULTS TO DETERMINE YOUR RETURN ON INVESTMENT (ROI)

While the intention of this book is not to teach you all the elements of advertising, I will mention that when you include contact information in your copy, you create a way to track the effectiveness of your ad. This is where the use of a coupon or promotion is helpful. Not only is the concept of saving money always a great motivator in getting customers to act and buy products and services, but it also creates a great way to track the results of your ad. The call to action is often the tool used to measure the results of an advertisement or marketing campaign. It can help determine the effectiveness of the ad (including your copywriting) by making it measurable. A specific phone number to call, a coupon to use, or a promotional discount if the customer mentions the ad are examples of calls to action that are directly measurable and can help you determine your ROI to make future advertising or marketing decisions.

If you don't want to discount your product or service with a coupon or promotion, you can simply ask your customers how they heard about your product or service. While this method is not precise in determining how well your ad placement or copy performed, it provides enough information to help you plan your future advertising campaigns. In addition, it might help segue into a longer conversation with customers, which will help you further develop your customer demographic profile (Step 3 of the Copywriting Outline).

EXAMPLES OF *CALL TO ACTION* COPYWRITING

Following are examples of copy demonstrating how the addition of action-oriented phrases that create a sense of urgency and tell your customers how to act are more effective than passive copy.

Product: All Flooring—flooring materials and installation
Call to Action: store visit
Promotion: 30% off all laminate flooring purchased on December 31st

All Flooring wants to liquidate its laminate flooring inventory before the end of the year, so they intend to host a one-day sale on December 31st offering 30% off all laminate flooring purchased on that day. They are placing an ad in their local newspaper using copy that says, "All Flooring offers 30% off all laminate flooring purchased on December 31st." This copy certainly tells customers what All Flooring is offering, but it is missing the necessary call to action elements. Instead, the copy could say, "Hurry in! Visit All Flooring on December 31st and get 30% of Pergo Flooring. Huge discounts are only available on December 31st. Don't miss it! We're located next to Wal-Mart on Main Street (1-800-555-1111)." Now the copy is stuffed with action-oriented phrases that create a strong sense of urgency. It also provides a specific instruction telling customers how to act (clear directions for local residents to find the store).

This copy doesn't include a way to measure the effectiveness of the ad and the promotion, but the owner of All Flooring could easily add a way of measuring the results by revising the copy and telling customers to bring the ad in to receive the discount or mention it for free delivery or an alternate freebie. Small business owners with limited budgets need to determine if including a discount or promotion with an ad is appropriate for their business goals.

Product: Fences and More—residential fence installation
Call to action: phone number
Promotion: none

Fences and More wants to build its customer base in a development of new homes. They are sending a direct mail piece to each homeowner to increase awareness of their business among the new residents. The copy for the mailing says, "Adhering to quality standards, fences are installed professionally by Fences and More. Call us at 1-800-555-2222." This copy is a great example of the poor choice of using the passive voice in copywriting. By rewriting the copy it could say, "Fences and More installs your fence professionally and adheres to the most stringent quality standards in the industry. Call 1-800-555-2222 for your free estimate today." The new copy uses the active voice and creates a sense of urgency with the inclusion of "today."

Furthermore, even though Fences and More always provides free estimates, they can use this service as a promotional tool in their copy thereby making customers think they're getting something extra. While Fences and More is not offering a promotion or discount to help track their ad, they easily can ask prospective customers who call for a free estimate how they heard about Fences and More. They also can use these conversations to help track the effectiveness of their ad as well as build their target audience's demographic profile.

Product: Custom Baskets—gift baskets
Call to Action: phone number
Promotion: mention ad and get free upgrade to priority shipping

Imagine Custom Baskets is a home-based business that creates custom gift baskets for all occasions. Shortly before Mother's Day, the owner is placing an ad using copy that describes her baskets. Her copy closes with, "We're looking forward to doing business with you." This copy fails in two ways in terms of creating a call to action. First, it creates no sense of urgency. Second, it doesn't tell the customer what to do next. The copy could be rewritten to say, "Don't delay! Call 1-800-555-5555 to order today. Mention this ad and automatically get a free upgrade to priority shipping." Now the copy is significantly more effective. By rewriting the copy using the active voice, adding a sense of urgency, and telling customers what to do next (call a toll-free number), the ad is more action-oriented and more likely to compel customers to act. It also includes a promotion (free shipping) to aid in tracking the results.

 REAL-WORLD EXAMPLES

If you turn on your television, you'll most certainly see several local car dealership commercials that do a great job of creating a sense of urgency and including effective calls to action. A popular method used by car dealerships urges customers to hurry in to take advantage of a short-lived promotion like a President's Day sale or end-of-season price reduction. Some famous ad campaigns also provide great call to action examples. Nike's ad campaign that uses the line, "Just do it" is an ideal example. Nike isn't telling people to think about trying their product. They're telling them to *just do it*. That is, they're telling customers to buy and wear Nikes. Don't think about it. Just do it. Similarly, Cover Girl used an effective call to action in commercials for their Advanced Radiance Age-Defying makeup with copy that says, "Younger looking skin in a week? Why wait? How about in an instant?" This is a superb example of a call to action with a conversational tone.

Creating sales and promotions with specific end dates is a great way to develop effective calls to action. For example, I saw a commercial for Kohl's department store recently that hyped an in-store sale. The commercial used copy that said, "Last three days for the lowest prices of the season." In this copy, Kohl's successfully told customers to hurry in, so they wouldn't miss the limited-time, special sale prices. The call to action created a sense of urgency as well as a specific deadline.

While reading a business magazine recently, I came across an ad for SCORE (Counselors to America's Small Business supported by the U.S. Small Business Administration/SBA). The ad read, "Live your dream. SCORE can help. Grow your business today." By inviting the target audience of small business owners to grow their businesses *today*, SCORE created a sense of urgency to which their target audience would respond.

Another real-world example of effective call to action copy comes from a billboard I recently passed on the highway in Orlando, Florida. The billboard advertised the *Orlando Sentinel*, which is the largest newspaper in Central Florida. The copy simply said, "In-depth news everyday. Subscribe today." The call to action is very simply written as, "Subscribe today," but it is very effective in creating a sense of urgency and motivating the audience to take action and subscribe sooner rather than later.

SUMMARY

Use Step 8 of the Copywriting Outline to create a list of urgent phrases to implement in your copy. Also, determine what you want your customers to do after seeing your ads and then create a specific call to action message that effectively directs customers on how to act. Your calls to action may vary depending on the advertising medium, which may require you to create additional phrases to tell customers what they need to do next.

You'll also need to determine what kinds of promotions and discounts you want to offer for each of your products during specific times of the year and in specific media. Write copy to highlight these promotions and

CASE STUDY ABC TAX SERVICES

See Chapter 17 for the complete Copywriting Outline for ABC Tax Services as well as ad and marketing collateral samples using copy culled from the Copywriting Outline.

Copywriting Outline Step 8

Step 8: Include a Call to Action—What is my call to action? What do I want my customers to do as soon as they read my ad? How can I create a sense of urgency?

- Call now.
- Stop by today.
- April 15th is almost here.
- Don't delay.
- It's tax time already.
- The IRS is waiting for your return.
- The clock is ticking.
- Get your refund fast.
- You've already waited long enough for that money.
- Don't wait any longer for your refund.

determine in advance how you plan to track each promotion to analyze its effectiveness. Finally, put these elements together along with the copy you created using Step 1 through Step 7 of the Copywriting Outline, review the entire piece, and where appropriate, change the copy that you wrote in the passive voice to the active voice to create the most compelling ad overall.

chapter eleven

step nine
C.Y.A.
(Cover Your Ass)

ONLY PROMISE WHAT YOU CAN DELIVER

Writing effective copy entails crafting compelling marketing messages, but it's essential to ensure you deliver on all promises offered in your ad or marketing piece. Never leave yourself or your business open to litigation or bad press by either touting claims that are only half truths or excluding important information from your copy. These tactics are considered deceptive advertising and are punishable by law. I'm not an expert in business law and detailing the ramifications of deceptive advertising is beyond the scope of this book. Suffice it to say, be honest in your copy. If your ad claims you have the lowest prices in town, do the research first and make sure your claim is accurate. Don't exaggerate about what your product or service can do for your customers. It's better to lose one sale than many because of negative word-of-mouth advertising from a dissatisfied customer. Being truthful gives you the opportunity to promote your business as honest

LEARNING OBJECTIVES

How to write copy that does not open you up to litigation

■

Words to use cautiously in copywriting

■

How to use disclaimers to back up the claims in your copy

and fair, which customers love to hear. In today's society, people are so used to being taken advantage of that a sincere business owner is rare and appreciated.

Be careful of using words like guarantee, lowest, best, or other superlatives such as the examples in the following list:

- Free
- Guaranteed
- Best, lowest, fastest, etc.
- Or your money back
- Risk-free
- No risk
- No purchase necessary
- No cost
- No obligation
- No investment
- 100%
- Promise
- No questions asked

Words and phrases like the examples previously listed are hard to prove and provide a perfect way for customers or competitors to question your claims. However, sometimes extreme adjectives are used subjectively. For example, it's hard to disprove a claim like, "We have the best salespeople," because the definition of the "best" salespeople varies from one consumer to another. Furthermore, anyone can claim to have the best salespeople, so using subjective copy like this is not the most effective way to use your limited advertising space. Superlatives are completely meaningless to con-

It's better to lose one sale than many because of negative word-of-mouth advertising from a dissatisfied customer.

sumers if they are not backed up with quantifiable evidence. For example, if a paint store owner claims to have the best paintbrushes, he needs to be certain that he does, in fact, carry the best paintbrushes available on the market, and he should be able to support that claim with hard evidence like an article from *Consumer Reports* or another authoritative source. Bottom line, don't rely on superlatives to create claims that are meant to persuade your audience unless you can back them up and make them meaningful.

DISCLAIMERS ARE YOUR FRIENDS

A simple trick to cover yourself when you make claims or promises in your ad copy is to include disclaimers. Always disclose all necessary information so customers completely understand the requirements or circumstances of your product, promotion, claim, or offer. Disclaimers can appear at the end of your ad to provide any restrictions or other necessary information needed to protect you as the advertiser and business owner. When you advertise in print, it's important to make sure your disclaimers are in a readable type size and font. Don't try to hide disclaimers in small type or in an obscure location. If a customer or competitor files a lawsuit against you based on a questionable claim in your ad and the disclaimer is not legible, you'll probably lose. Just including a disclaimer isn't enough to cover you. Customers need to be able to read it, or it may be considered deceptive advertising or a bait and switch tactic.

Evaluate your copy for loopholes or areas of potential confusion.

In basic terms, a bait and switch tactic occurs when marketing copy communicates an offer from a business, but when a customer actually tries to take advantage of the offer, the business does not honor it or tries to switch the offer to one that is more beneficial to the business and less beneficial to the customer. An example is an ad for a restaurant that uses headline copy that says, "Get 10% off your next meal," with no disclaimer copy (or even illegible disclaimer copy). After a customer has eaten, she starts to pay for her meal and discovers that the restaurant requires a $25 minimum food purchase to get the discount. This practice is considered a bait and switch tactic because the customer was baited into visiting the restaurant with the 10% discount offer, but once the purchase was made she discovered that the discount was only offered on checks over $25. To avoid being called a bait and switch tactic, the restaurant's copy needed a disclaimer stating something like, "10% discount valid only on checks $25 and over." The business owner protects himself by clearly informing the customer of the offer and it's restrictions.

> As the copywriter and business owner, you're responsible for the copy in your ads and marketing pieces. Take that responsibility very seriously and make sure you're protected.

Disclaimers can be used to cover advertisers in many ways. For example, you can use disclaimers to indicate coupon or promotion expiration dates, or you may want to indicate that your claim of having the lowest prices in town is limited to a single zip code. You can be creative in developing disclaimers that allow you to effectively promote your product or business while protecting yourself at the same time. When in doubt, use the disclaimer, "Subject to change." This phrase can be your best friend when you're writing copy.

PROVE IT

Make sure you can prove anything you say in your copy—especially claims about competitors that are likely to be challenged. After all, you don't want to be named in one of the countless lawsuits that are filed each day across the United States. If you make a promise or claim in your advertising copy, make sure you're able to backup those promises and claims with hard evidence. Using the previous example again, if your copy claims that you have the lowest prices in town, be certain that claim can be proven or provide a disclaimer defining the parameters of the claim. As the copywriter and business owner, you're responsible for the copy that is ultimately published. Make sure you cover your ass!

EXAMPLES OF C.Y.A. COPYWRITING

Following are a few examples of copy showing how minor changes can help you protect yourself from litigation, bad press, or negative word-of-mouth advertising.

Product: Our Town Used Cars—used cars
Claim: 0% financing

Our Town Used Cars is offering a 0% financing option to customers and plans to advertise the promotion in a local newspaper using copy that says, "Buy your car today with 0% financing." The copy clearly tells customers what the financing promotion offers, but there is the possibility that some of the customers won't qualify for 0% financing. Therefore, using copy that simply says customers can buy a car today with 0% financing is deceptive. The 0% financing offer needs to be available to all customers, or the copy needs to be edited to protect Our Town Used Cars from a lawsuit filed by an angry customer who does not qualify. To cover themselves, Our Town Used Cars could revise the copy to say, "Buy your car today with 0% financing for qualified buyers." A more subtle option is to include an asterisk after, "Buy your new car today with 0% financing*," and include disclaimer copy stating, "*Subject to credit approval." It's up to the business owner to decide how obvious they want the restrictions to be in their ad, meaning whether the restrictions appear within the ad copy or with an asterisk separate from the main ad copy. The most important part is to include the restrictions somewhere in the ad, so it is not considered deceptive.

Product: Sunny Patios—outdoor furniture
Claim: 50% discount on lounge chairs

Sunny Patios is trying to sell their overstock by offering lounge chairs at a 50% discount during the July 4th weekend. They decide to place an ad in the local beach newsletter with copy that says, "Get 50% off all lounge chairs at Sunny Patios during the July 4th weekend." While the owner of Sunny Patios might think the copy is quite clear, there are customers who will try to take advantage of this kind of vague copy. To protect himself from opportunity seekers, the owner could include a disclaimer at the end of the ad that says, "Offer valid July 3rd and 4th on purchases made from Sunny Patios' in-stock lounge chairs. Not valid on prior purchases." Sunny Patio needs to make sure there is no room for customers to push the envelope and apply the discount to other products or prior sales, which would cause the business to lose money.

Product: Regal Furniture—residential furniture
Claim: free delivery

Regal Furniture offers free delivery for customers and always includes this offer in their ad copy by simply stating, "Free delivery." Unfortunately, the owners of Regal Furniture are leaving themselves open to problems because they have a predetermined radius in which they provide free delivery. Beyond this radius, they either charge a delivery fee or decline to make the delivery. While they have not experienced problems yet, it is possible that a customer will enter the store, purchase a couch, and ask Regal Furniture to deliver it to a location 300 miles away. Instead of inviting potential problems, Regal Furniture could revise their copy to include a disclaimer that says, "Free delivery within a 30 mile radius of the Regal Furniture store. Deliveries between 31–50 miles incur a $50 fee. Delivery is not available beyond 51 miles." With this disclaimer, Regal Furniture protects themselves by making their delivery policy very clear. Alternatively, Regal Furniture could use a generic disclaimer that says, "Subject to certain restrictions." This will give them the opportunity to work with each individual customer to determine appropriate delivery options or charges.

 ## REAL-WORLD EXAMPLES

A common disclaimer used by advertisers is, "While supplies last." Fast food restaurants often include this disclaimer when they advertise promotional toys that come with kids' meals. McDonald's also uses this phrase when advertising their annual Monopoly game, telling customers that game pieces are only available while supplies last and only at participating stores. Dunkin' Donuts used this type of disclaimer in a recent commercial advertising a promotion saying, "Prices and participation may vary." Sometimes companies include their disclaimers within the main copy of the ad to urge customers to hurry in, "While supplies last." Other companies include this copy in fine print. It's up to you as the small business owner to determine how you want to communicate the copy that provides your legal protection. Just remember to include it.

Diet products like TRIMSPA also include copy to cover the advertiser's ass. In fine print at the bottom of most diet products' ads, you'll find a disclaimer that says, "Results not typical," or a similar phrase. Since the actors used in diet commercials usually represent an extremely successful and unusual story, it's critical for the advertisers to protect themselves with disclaimers.

Car manufacturers are also heavy users of disclaimer copy. Not only do they often advertise special interest rates and financing programs that require a multitude of disclaimers to meet truth-in-lending laws, but they also frequently include disclaimers stating that pricing promotions are valid on specific models only. Disclaimers used by car manufacturers don't stop with interest rates and financing programs. I saw a Volvo S80 commercial that demonstrated a common disclaimer used by car manufacturers wherein the car in the commercial had every upgrade imagineable. To ensure that

CASE STUDY ABC TAX SERVICES

See Chapter 17 for the complete Copywriting Outline for ABC Tax Services as well as ad and marketing collateral samples using copy culled from the Copywriting Outline.

Copywriting Outline Step 9

Step 9: C.Y.A. (Cover Your Ass)—What are some phrases I want to remember to include in my ads to protect myself? Is there anything else I need to remember to back up my claims?

- **Confidence Guarantee:** Up to 10%, excluding withholdings for IRS or medical debt or other liens against the refund.

- **Audit protection:** For a maximum of one year from the date of first contact regarding the audit from the IRS, a representative will be available via telephone for consultation and will attend one face-to-face meeting with the IRS (taxpayer responsible for travel expenses).

customers understood that high-end rims, leather seats, and other options were not included in the advertised price, the disclaimer, "Optional equipment," was added. Furthermore, a recent BMW commercial showing one of their cars being driven in a dangerous manner used a disclaimer that said, "Professional driver. Closed course." Often, car companies also include disclaimers about government crash test results and warnings about wearing seat belts and avoiding drinking and driving.

These are all common examples of car manufacturers and dealerships covering their asses with carefully crafted disclaimers. Some industries, like financial services and pharmaceuticals, are required to make more disclaimers than others. Frequently, prescription drug ads will include a disclaimer that says, "Available by prescription only," as well as a plethora of other required legal disclaimers. Again, as a small business owner, you'll need to determine what to disclose in your ads to ensure that you are not exposed to potential lawsuits.

SUMMARY

While large companies have legal departments that review copy to ensure it does not expose the company to potential problems, smaller companies don't usually have the budget to seek the opinion of an attorney for each ad they run or marketing piece they print. However, that doesn't mean small business owners have any less responsibility for producing ads and marketing pieces that are honest and not considered deceptive. Most small business owners are sole proprietors meaning if they lose a lawsuit, not only can their business assets be used to satisfy a plaintiff's claim, but their personal assets can be targeted as well. When you're writing copy, consider if claims that you can't prove in your copy (or can't provide appropriate disclaimers for) are worth it once you weigh the risk vs. the potential reward.

Aside from opening yourself up to possible litigation, exaggerating or falsifying claims about your product or your competition is unethical and a bad business practice. If you're caught in a lie (no matter how small) word will spread quickly, and your reputation could be irreparably damaged. Again, weigh the risk vs. the potential reward before you advertise using claims you can't prove.

chapter twelve

step ten
Proofread

SPELLING AND GRAMMATICAL ERRORS = WASTED ADVERTISING DOLLARS

It is critical that you accurately proofread your copy. One of the quickest ways to lose credibility in advertising is to allow grammatical or spelling errors to appear in your advertisement or marketing pieces. Customers translate carelessness in ads into carelessness in products and service. They ask themselves, "If this company doesn't care enough to produce an ad without errors, how likely are they to care about taking care of me?" Professional businesses produce professional quality ads and ad copy, and that means their copy has been proofread again and again and is error free.

Not everyone is a spelling and grammar expert. In fact, many people think they are terrible spellers. How then can small business owners ensure their copy does not include grammatical or spelling errors? It's simple. Use the tools available to you to make sure your ad contains no spelling

LEARNING OBJECTIVES

What tools to use to help you proofread your copy

■

How to write conversational copy

■

Which grammatical rules can be broken in copywriting

> Proofreading errors equate to a lack of professionalism in consumers' minds.

errors and is grammatically correct. These tools include a dictionary as well as automatic Spell Check and Grammar Check in your word processing application. Doing a simple online search for "grammar" through your preferred search engine will provide a wealth of online resources to help you correctly structure sentences. Once you've exhausted your personal proofreading efforts, ask friends, relatives, or colleagues to review your copy for errors.

Almost every writer knows that the worst person to proofread an ad or other written piece is themselves. The rule is to never proofread your own work. Of course, with a limited budget, small business owners have to wear many hats including copywriter and proofreader. That's why using the tools available to you, as well as recruiting friends and relatives to help you, are essential parts of successful proofreading for small business owners.

IT'S TIME TO WALK AWAY

When you complete your copy, take a break before you begin proofreading it. One of the biggest proofreading mistakes is to immediately switch your writer's hat to your proofreader's hat. If you're going to have any chance of catching your own grammatical and spelling errors, it's critical that you step away from your work before you edit it. This break will allow you to take a look at your copy with a fresh eye, so you'll be better inclined to tighten it using the Red Pen Rule that we discussed in Step 7 of the Copywriting Outline.

BE CONVERSATIONAL

The tone of "voice" of your copy should match your product *and* your audience. You just learned that proper grammar is essential in copywriting to ensure that your business looks professional. At the same time, you don't want to come across as arrogant, and you don't want to sound like you're writing a paper for your high school English class.

While avoiding glaring grammatical errors is critical, don't worry about perfect grammar. You don't want to sacrifice a conversational, welcoming tone for flawless grammar. For example, while you were probably taught that contractions have no place in formal writing, it's the first rule you should ignore in copywriting. Furthermore, I remember my English teacher adamantly telling us that a preposition should never be left dangling at the end of a sentence. Ignore that rule, too. There are some grammatical rules that can make your advertising copy difficult to read or too formal. Breaking rules is okay as long as it makes your copy flow better and sound more appealing to your target audience.

It's OK to break grammar rules if doing so makes your copy sound natural and conversational.

The manner in which you structure your sentences and paragraphs also has a strong impact on the effectiveness of your copy. People typically skim an advertisement or marketing piece rather than reading it word-for-word (despite what copywriters might like to think). Therefore, short sentences and short paragraphs are more compelling than long blocks of text. Don't be afraid to use sentence fragments or paragraphs made up of just one sentence regardless of grammar rules. Remember, an ad or marketing piece only has seconds to capture a customer's attention and only seconds more to keep that person reading. The structure of your copy should work in tandem with the design of your ad or marketing piece to keep the audience following the path you've laid out for them.

DON'T LOSE SALES WITH POOR SPELLING AND GRAMMAR

If you want to see real-world examples of copy with spelling and grammatical errors, browse through some eBay or Craigslist listings. It seems like the majority of the ads on those two websites were not proofread. From

🔍 CLOSEUP

Examples of Acceptable Grammatical Rule-Breaking for Copywriting
- Write copy to sound conversational, not formal
- Use contractions
- End sentences with prepositions
- Use sentence fragments
- Use one-sentence paragraphs
- Use colloquialisms and slang words

my own experience, I'm more likely to pass on a listing that was carelessly written and edited. I simply don't trust the seller, and I'd rather spend a few dollars more on another item from a seller who spent the time to produce a listing that was well written. At the very least, it takes just a few minutes for an advertiser to read through a listing to catch the glaring mistakes. Each error is a reflection of the seller. The same holds true for any business owner producing advertisements or marketing materials. What image do you want to portray? Make sure your copy reflects that image. Your image and the role of branding will be discussed in further detail in Chapter 14.

EXAMPLES OF *PROOFREADING*

The following examples demonstrate how different spelling and/or grammatical errors can detract from your message and hurt the response rate for your ad. Of course, a lower response rate means fewer sales and wasted advertising dollars, so proofread, proofread, proofread! Then proofread again.

Product: West Florida Bed and Breakfast—
Florida hotel accommodations

The West Florida Bed and Breakfast is placing an ad in a travel magazine targeting vacationers. They produce an ad that says, "Visit Florda today." This is an example of a classic proofreading error, which is very common when the author is the sole proofreader. Often people read a word that is misspelled but see it the way it's supposed to be spelled. Their minds play tricks on them because it's a word with which they're very familiar. It seems like a minor error, but from customers' perspectives, it's a glaring mistake. In fact, it's laughable. If I saw this ad, my first thought would be, "They can't even correctly spell the name of their own state?" Next, I would question the attention to detail and service provided by the bed and breakfast, and I would be wary of choosing this location for my next vacation. Of course, as a copywriter, I may be overly sensitized to proofreading errors in ads, but I think most customers would agree with me on this one.

Product: Mike's Car Repair Shop—automotive repairs

Mike's Car Repair Shop is placing an ad in the local newspaper to attract new customers. Mike, the owner, wants to highlight some of the shop's services in the ad, and remembering that sentences should never end with prepositions, he writes, "When you choose Mike's Car Repair Shop, you'll have nothing about which to worry." Yes, Mike followed an important grammatical rule, but his copy sounds like it came out of a high school English text book instead of being conversational and engaging. That's not the tone Mike wants to convey to his target audience.

Instead, Mike should revise his copy to read, "When you choose Mike's Car Repair Shop, you'll have nothing to worry about." While the sentence now has a dangling preposition, it's more conversational and has a friendlier tone. Mike can follow this sentence with a list of his services and tie them back to his peace-of-mind claim thereby creating a welcoming tone with a concise message that will drive customers to action.

Product: Yummy Bakery—fresh baked goods

Yummy Bakery wants to place an ad in the local paper to hype the freshness and quality of their home-baked goods. They print copy that says, "Yummy Bakery knows your too busy to bake and bakery items from the grocery store are just not good enough so we bake all of our items fresh each day." There are a few spelling and grammar errors in this example. First, "your" should be in its possessive form (you're). Second, this is a run-on sentence. Yummy Bakery should fix the grammatical and spelling errors in their copy to say, "Yummy Bakery knows you're too busy to bake yourself, but you want the freshness and quality of homemade. Don't settle for bakery items from the grocery store. Every item at Yummy Bakery is made fresh in our kitchen each day and goes straight from our oven to your table." Grammatical and spelling errors in the original copy not only detract from Yummy Bakery's image, but the copy is also difficult to read. By revising the copy to fix these errors, Yummy Bakery appears more professional and is more likely to boost sales with compelling, action-oriented copy.

 REAL-WORLD EXAMPLES

Some of the most famous ad campaigns include a conversational tone, and as a result, they include grammatical errors. For example, the famous copy for 7UP that referred to the soda as, "The Uncola," included an obvious error. Uncola is not a word. 7UP used a word that is not in the dictionary to refer to its product. This is a great example of how some spelling and grammatical errors can be justified when they help make your tone conversational or add to the style of your ad campaign.

CASE STUDY ABC TAX SERVICES

See Chapter 17 for the complete Copywriting Outline for ABC Tax Services as well as ad and marketing collateral samples using copy culled from the Copywriting Outline.

Copywriting Outline Step 10

Step 10: Proofread—Who can proofread my ad for me? What tools are available to help me proofread my ad?

- Employees
- Spell check
- Dictionary
- Attorney

Brylcreem had an extremely successful and famous campaign that said, "A little dab'll do ya." This copy includes two glaring errors—"dab'll" and "ya." However, the style of the ad concept and conversational tone made these errors appropriate and welcomed. Grammatical errors for the sake of creating a conversational tone should never be permitted if they detract from your ad, but if they enhance it—go for it.

Recently, I saw a great example of copywriting that breaks a well known grammar rule to create a more conversational tone. The ad appeared in a parenting magazine and advertised Pure Protein bars. The main copy read, "Eat good. Look great." The copy includes a glaring grammatical error. The word "good" in the first sentence should be replaced with "well." The copywriter intentionally included this error to create a bigger impact for the ad. The word "good" is a double entendre. It refers to the taste of the protein bars as well as the healthiness of the bars. Without the grammatical error, the copy would lose its meaning and would not work as effectively.

SUMMARY

The easiest way to nullify your advertising efforts and throw your advertising budget out the window is to produce ads or marketing materials that include unintentional spelling and grammatical errors. While you don't need to be a slave to your high school grammar textbook, you should use a dictionary and ask another person to proofread your copy. You're spending a lot of money to place and print your ad or marketing piece. Don't waste it with substandard quality proofreading.

chapter thirteen

Common Forms of Copywriting

As discussed in Chapter 8, the copy you write is largely dependent on the media in which your advertisement or marketing piece appears. While a thorough analysis of copywriting in each medium is beyond the scope of this book, following is an overview of commonly used media as well as some copywriting tips for each.

PRINT ADVERTISING AND MARKETING COLLATERAL

When you think of print advertising, the first thing that probably comes to mind is magazine advertising or newspaper advertising. Placing ads in periodicals and newspapers is certainly a common way to advertise a business, product, or service, but there are actually many print media in which a company can communicate its marketing message. Following is a list of some of the more common print media.

Print Ads

Magazines ads are often thought of as the crème de la crème of print advertising simply because they can be visually stunning and very expensive. There are often less expensive options for small businesses in regional magazines and trade periodicals. Print advertising opportunities can be even more affordable in newspapers and local telephone books. The copywriter's role is to craft messages that work well in the specific medium in which the ad will appear.

Print advertisements vary significantly from the amount of space offered to the ad spend amount. A full-page ad provides more space for text than a quarter-page ad. However, don't fall into the trap of trying to fill up a print ad with text. Print ads are often placed near text heavy articles, so the comparative white space in a print ad can have a profound visual effect and draw consumers further into your message. Graphics and a strong headline also play a critical role in capturing the attention of the audience who is probably not looking at the magazine or newspaper for the ads but rather for the articles.

Outdoor Advertising

Just say "no" to cluttered ads.

Outdoor advertising comes in the form of billboards, posters, signs, and more. The medium is reliant on quick messages that are seen and understood in just seconds. This means that the corresponding copy needs to be succinct. There is simply no room for filler words or extraneous information. Typically, outdoor advertising is most effective when it contains a single message. For example, consumers driving on the highway at 65 mph can't read more than just a few words on a billboard ad, so the words need to be effective and memorable.

Point-of-Sale Collateral and Signage

Banners, posters, window decals, in-store displays, mobiles, tent cards, counter cards, and more are used to grab the attention of consumers when they're ready to make a purchase at the checkout line or counter. The offer, message, and copy used on point-of-sale collateral needs to be timely and action oriented. Make sure point-of-sale messages are accurate and appropriately placed. For example, if you were standing in line at the checkout counter of your grocery store and saw a sign that said, "All magazines half price," you might very well toss a magazine you like on the conveyor belt. However, if the sign said, "Coke 12-packs half price," you would be less likely to step out of line and walk back to the soft drinks section to get a 12-pack of Coke. In-store messages need to speak directly to consumers at the moment they see them, so they can act at that moment.

> Remember the Hook and Reel Technique: Use copy to catch a customer's attention (the hook) then draw him or her in to read or listen further (the reel), then do it over and over until you've landed that customer.

Marketing Handouts

Brochures and flyers are typically distributed to consumers to provide additional information about a product or service. They provide more space to communicate multiple messages and graphics. Many copywriters fall into the trap of including too much text on marketing handouts. Even a lengthy capabilities brochure can be too detailed. Remember the Red Pen Rule. Every element of copy should add value to the overall message. White space is not the enemy.

Additionally, most people will not read a brochure cover to cover. With that in mind, treat each new page as a new ad (if your layout allows it). That means you should use headlines, callouts, pull quotes, and other design techniques to draw your audience into each new page, just like you're trying to catch their attention for a brand new ad or marketing piece. People get bored quickly. Keep hooking them and reeling them in again and again.

TELEVISION AND RADIO

Television and radio ads are different from print ads and marketing materials simply because there is such a heavy dependence on visual appeal and audio appeal. Your message should be short and to the point, and make sure you repeat it. Customers who see or hear a television or radio ad may not have the chance to double-check a message they missed, so you need to ensure they hear your message by repeating it more than once. This is particularly important for your ad's call to action. Also, work closely with your design team to create a concept, image, and audio that enhances your message rather than confusing it or detracting from it.

DIRECT RESPONSE

Direct Mail

Direct mail is meant to communicate directly to the recipient. Therefore, personalization is important. Personalization usually depends on budgetary constraints, but it's important to try to personalize each mail piece at least in the address and greeting areas. That's just one way to help your mail piece stand out among the mountain of mail, junk mail, and offers consumers receive in their mailboxes everyday.

There are three main elements of successful direct-mail copywriting:

1. **The teaser:** Teaser messages are used on direct-mail envelopes to hook the recipient and tempt them to open the envelope. Teasers are used again in the headlines, callouts, and sidebars to keep the recipient reading.

2. **The offer:** Generally, the offer is the most important element of your direct-mail piece, but another effective technique is to entice your audience before they see the offer. Consider your audience, the offer, and its details before determining where to present the offer in your direct-mail piece.

3. **The details:** The details of your piece are what will convince your customers that they cannot live without your offer. From touting benefits to hyping differentiators and appealing to emotional triggers, the details personalize the offer for the recipient. The details tell the recipient W.I.I.F.M. (What's In It For Me).

Similar to copywriting for brochures, don't fall into the trap of providing too much information in a direct-mail piece simply because the space is there. Frequently, I receive direct-mail pieces that are so cluttered, it's impossible to even find the offer or call to action, let alone be teased into reading more. Remember the K.I.S.S. rule and avoid T.M.I. when you're writing direct mail copy.

Email

Email marketing can be more budget friendly than traditional direct mail, but it does have drawbacks, not the least of which is trying to get your message *delivered* through the various spam blockers available today. Your copy can make or break your email campaign's ability to get to your recipients' inboxes. With that in mind, following is a list of words and phrases to use with caution in your email message subject lines because they are commonly considered spam by detection software, which will relegate your message to the spam folder before your audience even reads it.

- Don't delete
- Please read
- Not spam
- Free
- You're a winner
- Congratulations
- Guarantee
- Save money
- Information you requested
- No fees
- Amazing
- Promise
- Credit
- Loan
- Order now
- Click to remove
- No risk
- Offer
- Opportunity
- Urgent

Craft email marketing messages so they contain useful and timely information your recipients want and need. Write a personalized message that speaks directly to the specific consumer who receives the message and then tease the recipient to keep reading. Your offer should be presented early in the email message so readers don't have to scroll to find it. It's important that the copy hooks readers without asking them to scroll first.

Telemarketing

Telemarketing is a tough sell these days due to the various laws and regulations related to the National Do Not Call Registry. If you are called upon to write copy for a telemarketing campaign, use a conversational tone that matches your audience. Present the offer early to intrigue the customer to inquire about additional details. Keeping a person on the phone who did not ask to be called is a difficult task. Don't give customers the chance to hang up by focusing on extraneous details before you present your offer. Avoid T.M.I.

> Copy must be timely and up-to-date to be effective.

ONLINE MARKETING

Banner Ads and Text Ads

Online ads are most similar to outdoor advertising and point-of-sale display ads for two reasons. First, there is little time or space to include a comprehensive message. Like a billboard or poster, online users move quickly and an online ad needs to capture their attention even more quickly. The goal of most online ads is to motivate the consumer to click through to another website where they can make a purchase, request additional information, or gain awareness. With that in mind, offers need to be timely and appropriate for where and when they will be seen. More than once, I've been served an online banner ad for an offer that already expired. Make sure your copy moves faster than the internet.

Websites

You can direct customers to your website by including your URL in your advertising and marketing efforts as part of your call to action. A website can be a static source for information about your company and products or it can be a transactional destination. You could have an online store available at your website with appropriate copy tied to each product you're trying to sell. A static site acts somewhat like an online brochure but with more interactivity than the print medium offers (users participate by following links). Static websites also provide the opportunity to communicate the most current information about your product, business, or promotions because there is no printing lag time.

When you write copy for the web, it's important to understand search engine optimization. Use keywords and links so search engines find your site and help drive traffic to your site and boost your business. Depending on the nature of your business, using a conversational tone can be more effective than a using a strictly professional tone. The web is an interactive medium, and it makes sense to use an interactive, conversational tone to attract new customers. Keep sentences and paragraphs short. Pay attention to white space to provide visual relief from text-heavy pages. Use headlines and graphics to tease visitors to read more and link deeper into the website.

Use the appropriate tone and voice to appeal to your audience but stay true to your overall brand image at the same time.

Have you ever been searching for something online, started reading, and looked at the clock only to find hours have passed since you started? I call that *Internet Time*, and it's like a vortex. You get sucked in and don't realize how much time you've been surfing until you've wasted half your day. That's how you want visitors on your site to feel. You want to hook them again and again and keep them reading by providing compelling messages that speak directly to them.

Blogs and Social Media Marketing

Web 2.0 is still evolving as the social web. Instead of websites simply providing static information, communities and networks are the hot online trend in the 21st century. Even corporate marketers have yet to harness the power of the social web, but small businesses can leverage its impact simply by joining the online conversation. Writing a blog, commenting on other blogs, and joining in discussions on social media sites such as Facebook and

LinkedIn can all be effective ways to market your business. Your communications through these social web tools are extensions of your brand message and therefore should be written with copywriting in mind. For example, starting a blog for your company means more than just publishing posts about events in your industry and regurgitating corporate rhetoric. It means writing posts with your brand image and message in mind and relating these posts to your business and your customers. Use your copywriting skills to make these posts meaningful to your current and prospective customers to further promote your brand and business.

Unlike websites, blogs provide a truly interactive, conversational experience for customers and can be updated faster and easier than static websites. Blogs also help drive more traffic to your static website or online store because they typically rank high in online searches by Google, Yahoo!, or other search engines. We'll discuss blogs and the social web in more detail in Chapter 14.

OTHER ADVERTISING AND MARKETING OPPORTUNITIES

There are a variety of marketing tactics that rely on effective copywriting to ensure success. Following is a short list of some of these tactics and how compelling copy can make them more effective.

Newsletters

Newsletters are an effective marketing tool if they contain articles and copy that are meaningful to their readers. Many newsletters fail because their content is simply a regurgitation of the company's accomplishments and provide little added value to consumers. Copywriting for newsletters is just like copywriting for other marketing materials. Remember to keep your target audience in mind as you craft your message. What's in it for them when they read your newsletter? Make sure the content benefits the audience who reads it and compels them to want to do business with you. A newsletter by name is "newsy," but as a business communication tool, it also should be "salesy" and communicate your marketing message.

Billing Inserts, Billing Messages, and On Hold Messages

Monthly bills and invoices provide a perfect place to include a marketing message. Choose your message to match the tone of the billing process. Similarly, you can play recorded messages that are timely and appropriate while customers are on hold to boost sales. For example, your hold message could tell customers to ask about a new program that will help them save money or a new product that will help them save time. Don't forget to tie the benefits directly to the audience.

Press Releases

Press releases are used to develop publicity and word-of-mouth marketing around your business, product, or service. Write them so you're not just communicating an event like a journalist, but you're also hyping the benefits of your product and business. You want to drum up a buzz about your product as well as drive sales. Incorporate your marketing message into the latter part of your press release after you've already made your announcement. Using quotes from key figures in your industry or your customers helps emphasize and legitimize your message and your press release as a whole.

Speeches and Sales Presentations

Every speaking opportunity related to your business, service, or product is an opportunity to drive sales. From a speech at a local entrepreneurs association meeting to a sales pitch to a desirable new client, you have the chance to communicate your marketing message through well-crafted copy. Depending on the audience, you'll want to massage your marketing message to be more subtle or more obvious. Either way, target your message to your audience and relate that message directly to your audience's lives to get the biggest bang for your buck.

Coupons, Contests, and Special Promotions

There are so many different marketing strategies and tactics that a business can use to promote its products and services. Special coupon offers, contests, and promotions are common tactics that you can hype with compelling copywriting. Your copy for these types of marketing programs needs to show customers why the offers are special and why customers need to take advantage of them. This type of copy needs to focus on a sense of urgency and use emotional triggers to drive a perceived need that leads customers to action.

Giveaways, Promotional Items, and Incentive Items

Promotional and incentive items are typically given to consumers to further promote a business. These giveaway items come in a variety of forms such as pens, magnets, T-shirts, and more. The purpose of giveaways is to keep a business' name, contact information, and benefits in front of the customer. That means you should make sure each giveaway you invest in communicates your advertising and marketing message to deliver an adequate return on your investment. Of course, incentive items come in all shapes and sizes, which means you'll need to adjust your message to work within the space provided. For example, if you plan to giveaway a pen, printing your company name and phone number or website address might be all you can include simply because of the limited space. However, a refrigerator magnet provides enough room to print your contact information as well as some benefits and a call to action. Invest your promotional budget on items that your target audience is likely to respond to and will allow you to communicate your most compelling message.

 **SUMMARY**

Clearly, the copy you write must change based on the medium in which you're placing your ad or marketing piece. The important thing to remember is to write copy that fits the medium but also speaks directly to the target audience who sees it. Furthermore, maintain brand consistency by using similar messages across various media and remember to proofread! Follow the steps in the Copywriting Outline, apply them to the medium in which you're advertising, and you'll be on your way to boosting sales and profits with effective, compelling copy.

chapter fourteen

Copywriting, Blogging, and the Social Web

JUMPING ON THE BLOGGING BANDWAGON

It seems like business blogging is becoming a "must" these days as the social web takes a front seat in terms of generating word-of-mouth advertising both online and offline. We discussed websites and blogs briefly in Chapter 13, but blogging is still a new territory to many small and medium-size businesses. With that in mind, this chapter will introduce blogging as another element of the marketing toolkit that can benefit from targeted, consistent, and appropriate copywriting.

The power of viral marketing and the social web cannot be ignored, and every business should invest the time, energy, and budget necessary to determine if a business blog will add value to their customers' experiences with their companies, brands, products, and services. The argument can be made that every business will benefit from a blog. While that's probably true, it's still important to understand the role a blog plays in your business plan. A blog is different from a static website. Rather than simply providing information, a blog is a social medium. It invites participation and conversation between readers and helps drive an emotional involvement among consumers of your brand and products that ultimately will lead to customer loyalty, word-of-mouth marketing, and increased sales.

It's also important to understand that starting a blog and maintaining it is very inexpensive and very easy. While a website requires specific technical skills to create and update, a blog can be maintained by a person with extremely limited technical know-how. Since a blog is updated frequently and a new entry point is created with each new posting, search engines will pick up these postings quicker, making it easier and more likely that people searching for keywords related to your business will have a better chance of finding your blog (and thus your website, online store, etc.). This is the equivalent of increased store traffic for a retail brick-and-mortar store, and it leads to more sales opportunities generated from a minimal monetary investment.

A blog (a fusion of web and log) is a website that includes entries (called posts) that appear in reverse chronological order.

Before we go any further, let's talk about what a blog truly is. It's not a static website, but instead it is constantly changing. The best blogs are updated frequently, sometimes several times a day, with fresh content that keeps readers coming back for more. Blogs began as online diaries in which individuals shared their thoughts and opinions about their daily lives, but the power of the social interaction that blogs provided quickly grew in strength. Businesses noticed that creating a relationship with their customers through the two-way conversation that blogs invited was a catalyst to driving sales by meeting customer needs and creating customer loyalty. Customers no longer thought they were being "talked at." Instead, customers felt involved and important. The internet moved from being strictly informational and transactional to being highly social, and thus, Web 2.0 was born. User-generated content became the norm, and the power of the blogosphere grew.

Embracing the social web and engaging customers through a business blog is a simple way to not only communicate with your customers but to also promote your business in unique ways. Many large and small companies have entered the blogosphere in an attempt to harness the power of the social web, but marketers are still learning how best to leverage the reach and influence of user-generated content. Companies such as Wal-Mart, Dell, and General Motors each manage popular company blogs that are meant to bring customers closer to their brands. The recipe for success has yet to be fully defined, but one thing is for certain, the social web is the place to be. The best way to join the social web as a business owner is with a business blog.

WRITING A BUSINESS BLOG

Before you launch your business blog, you need to define your goals for it. From colors, to fonts, to functionality, and everything in between, you need to know the objectives for your business blog and every part of your blog needs to work together to help meet these objectives as well as consistently communicate your brand message and image. For example, a blog for a children's store would work well with playful colors and fonts, while a blog for an investment company should use more professional colors and fonts that are more closely associated with finance and stability.

While the design of your blog needs to consistently convey your brand image and message, so does your blog's content. Using the example above, if you own a children's store, your blog's tone should be friendly and fun; in contrast, an investment firm's blog should be far more professional with a serious tone that instills a sense of expertise and security to readers. In short, your tone needs to match your brand image. Branding is all about setting and meeting customer expectations. Your business blog is an important part of your brand strategy that should enhance and further communicate your brand promise—not detract from it or confuse it.

The content on your business blog is also dependent on your audience. Write content to attract visitors who resemble your best customers (as discussed in Step 3 of the Copywriting Outline) to generate the highest chance for sales conversion and loyalty. As your blog grows and attracts more loyal readers, take some time to analyze who those people are and create demographic profiles of the target audience for your blog. Then write content that meets the needs of that audience.

The most popular blogs are those where the blogger (the author) writes in a personable, unique voice that really connects with his or her audience. By voice I mean not just the tone of the content but also the personality that shines through it. Avoid writing like a reporter who is simply reciting the news. Instead, speak from the heart and inject your personality into your blog. That's what will intrigue readers, and that's what will keep them coming back again and again to read more of what you have to say.

Remember, blogging is about creating a two-way, social conversation. If you're speaking with someone who is simply speaking *at* you, how do you react? Most likely, you try to get away from that person and avoid them in the future, so you're not stuck listening to them drone on and on again. However, if you are speaking with someone who wants to hear what you have to say, asks you to participate, has interesting things to discuss with a unique point of view, responds to you, and is ultimately enjoyable to speak with, you are more likely to seek that person out in the future to speak with them again.

Your blog's goal is to create unique content that attracts new visitors and then keeps them there by engaging them in interesting and enjoyable conversations (the Hook and Reel Technique is discussed in Chapter 13). This, in turn, will lead to positive word-of-mouth marketing as your visitors tell others about your blog. As a result, your blog and business will grow.

WHAT TO WRITE ABOUT

Once you've decided to start a business blog, you need to determine what to write about. There are a few important things to keep in mind as you write a business blog. First, don't reiterate information that can be found on your website or other materials. The key to a successful blog is offering added value above and beyond what visitors can get anywhere else. For example, your business blog could provide educational information demonstrating how to use your products. Alternatively, you could offer exclusive information and tips or publish reviews of your products by customers or industry experts. You could also respond to customer questions and concerns through your blog or post customer or client success stories. Try to write a mixture of *evergreen* posts (posts that will remain relevant and useful) as well as timely posts that will keep your blog current, fresh, and unique.

"It's all about the content." This phrase is often cited as the most important rule of developing a successful blog.

There are many ways to bring added value to your customers' experiences on your blog. As you write your business blog posts, think about how you would verbally explain your business. What would you tell customers? These are the same subjects you should write about on your business blog. Provide information that makes readers feel like you're helping them, listening to them, teaching them, and interacting with them, and they will respond.

Avoid corporate rhetoric on your business blog. It's bad enough that employees have to sit through cheerleading sessions from their companies' human resources and public relations departments, don't make your customers listen to them, too. People are busy and they only have time to read blogs that bring them added value and actually provide helpful or entertaining information. Don't just regurgitate your first quarter results on your blog. Remember Step 4 of the Copywriting Outline, W.I.I.F.M? (What's In It For Me?). Give your visitors content they care about and can apply directly to their own lives, and they'll come back. Bore them with news of how wonderful your company is, and they'll move on.

It's also essential that you write with the same rules and ethics in mind that you would if you were writing in any other medium. Make sure you cite your sources and don't share insider information. Also, don't mention customers, clients, or vendors by name without their consent. While the laws of the internet are not as clear as laws related to other media, it's always best to err on the side of caution. Don't forget Step 9 of the Copywriting Outline, Cover Your Ass. It also applies to business blogging.

WORDS STAY ALIVE ONLINE

A fundamental truth about the internet is that anything published online today lives for a very long time. For example, if you have a negative interaction with a customer on a blog, user forum, or other website, it's highly likely that your customers will find that content for many years to come through search engines. Something you write online today may still be found online ten years from now. Keep that in mind as you post anything online using your name or your business' name.

Every time your name or your business' name appears online is another touch point for your customers to find you and learn about you. There are actually companies that focus on helping businesses and people in this area, called search engine reputation management (SERM). Remember, your online brand is very dependent on your online presence. Make sure when people search for you, your brand, or your company, the results are positive and enhance your brand image (or online reputation) rather than detract from it.

MARKETING YOUR BLOG

Blogging isn't just about writing content. If you want to use your blog as a sales tool to generate customers and sales, then you need to help people find it by marketing it. This means you'll need to spend time visiting and commenting on blogs where your potential customers are likely to be found. You'll also need to participate in the same online user forums as your customers and other social web activities, which may include social networking through sites such as Facebook and LinkedIn and social bookmarking through sites like Digg and StumbleUpon. It takes time to develop an online presence, find people who might be interested in reading your blog, encourage them to come back again, and tell other people about your blog. By participating in the social web, writing compelling content on your blog, and keeping your blog's content fresh, your blog will grow over time. It's important to be patient and not give up too soon.

THE PROS AND CONS OF HIRING A PROFESSIONAL BUSINESS BLOGGER

Let's face it. Writing and effectively marketing a blog is very time consuming. As a business owner, you may not have time to commit to blogging on a daily basis. Remember, successful blogs are updated frequently, sometimes more than once each day.

Web 2.0 (called the social web) is considered to be the second generation of the World Wide Web where content moved from being strictly informational and transactional to focusing on social interaction through user-generated content, networking, sharing, and community-building.

Before you undertake starting a business blog, you need to be able to commit to not only writing a blog post everyday but also responding to comments and marketing the blog. There is no point in starting a business blog unless it can be maintained and marketed. If you're able to commit to writing the content for your blog, then make sure you spend time studying everything you need to know to derive the most return from your blogging investment. This includes learning not only how to blog effectively, but also search engine optimization, blog marketing, and much more.

If you don't have time to learn how to fully optimize your business blog, then hiring a professional blogger might be a perfect choice. Most professional bloggers work from their homes as independent contractors, which means you don't have to pay for office space, taxes, or benefits. Professional bloggers know how to create a successful blog. They have the experience needed to immediately start writing compelling content, interact with the social web, promote and market your blog, optimize it for search engines, and more. If you decide to hire a professional blogger, make sure you have a complete understanding of that person's blog writing, social networking, blog marketing, and search engine optimization experience before you hire him or her. Not all professional bloggers are the same. Experience means a lot when it comes to hiring a blogger who can actually help you grow your business through your blog.

SUMMARY

Before you start a business blog, define your objectives and determine whether or not you have the time and energy required to make a blog successful. While a blog is an inexpensive marketing investment in terms of dollars, it does require an enormous amount of sweat equity to be successful. Your long-term goals for your blog will help you determine whether or not you should hire a professional blogger to help you.

It's equally critical that you determine the appropriate design and tone based on your overall brand promise before you launch a business blog. You need to live that promise across the web, everywhere your online presence appears. Success comes from consistency in terms of voice, creating fresh content, promoting and marketing, and interacting with readers and other bloggers. Consistency in those areas will lead to overall brand consistency, which in turn, will lead customers to develop an emotional involvement to your brand and, ultimately, create customer loyalty. Loyal customers talk about the products they are emotionally attached to and that word-of-mouth marketing from online influencers across the social web can lead to increased business for you and your company. Their reach is broad, and their power is strong. However, much of the influence of blogs has yet to be defined. One thing is for certain. In order for a blog to boost sales for you business, you need to be patient and give it time to grow.

chapter fifteen

Branding and Design

WHAT IS A BRAND?

What comes to mind when you think of a brand? Most people associate a brand with a company logo, such as the Nike swoosh, or a product name, like Starbucks, but logos and names are just two of the tangible parts of branding your business, service, product, or yourself. In truth, branding encompasses far more than just a graphic or word. Branding is the overall image you present in the marketplace and the way your customers perceive that image. In other words, you can try to create an image for your business or product, but ultimately, your brand depends on your customers' perceptions of it.

Let's look at an example of branding in more detail. What does the Hyundai brand mean to you? When you hear the Hyundai name or see the brand logo do you think of affordable cars? This is the brand image Hyundai portrays in the minds of consumers, and it identifies the brand's position in the marketplace. What if Hyundai released a luxury vehicle with a six-figure price tag? What would you think? You probably would think that a Hyundai luxury vehicle doesn't make any sense because the brand is perceived as inexpensive in the minds of consumers. After all, Hyundai makes sure the message of low cost is communicated in all of its marketing materials and advertising through consistent messaging.

Let's take a look at the way copy communicates Hyundai's brand message. Imagine that Hyundai launches a new ad campaign with copy that says, "Drive a Hyundai. Own the best." Does that copy consistently communicate the Hyundai brand message? Now imagine the copy is rewritten to say, "A comfortable ride at a comfortable price." The new copy is more appropriate for a Hyundai advertisement because it is consistent with the brand image of affordability that already exists in the mind of consumers. Rather than confusing customers, the new copy meets customers' expectations, thereby making it more acceptable to them.

Now imagine that Mercedes launches a new affordable vehicle priced under $20,000. This would run counter to the brand image Mercedes has worked so hard to create in people's minds. Consumers associate the Mercedes brand with a higher price tag and different clientele than those shopping at a Hyundai dealership. Mercedes successfully has built a brand image of high-end, luxury vehicles for discerning drivers. With that in mind, consider these two copy examples for Mercedes, "You deserve the best, and only Mercedes will do," vs. "Mercedes, the safe choice." Both of these copy examples are accurate, but which does a better job of consistently communicating the Mercedes brand image and message? My vote goes to the first example—it speaks to the target audience's emotional triggers of wanting to be leaders and keeping up with the Joneses. The second example seems better suited to a brand like Volvo, which is known primarily for its safety features.

Consistent branding creates customer expectations and drives customer loyalty.

What does this mean to you as a business owner or copywriter? It means that you need to decide your brand image before you begin advertising and

🔍 CLOSEUP

The Three Main Steps of Branding

1. **Define:** Carefully describe the desired image the brand will portray in the marketplace.

2. **Communicate:** Make sure consumers hear and understand your brand message.

3. **Be persistent and consistent:** Repeat your brand message again and again, communicating the same brand image every time.

marketing. (See the Closeup Box for the three main steps of branding.) Your company name, product name, and your logo are the tangible and visual representations of your brand image—every piece of your business should reflect that brand image including your advertisements, website, marketing materials, direct mail, business cards, letterhead, invoices, shopping bags, store displays, and so on. Use every opportunity possible to persistently communicate a consistent brand image.

BRANDING HELPS DRIVE CUSTOMER LOYALTY

You will increase the loyalty of your customers by creating your brand strategy up-front. The consistency of your brand image will help you meet what I call the Three S's of Customer Loyalty (see Closeup Box). Inconsistent messages in copywriting or business communications will confuse customers who inherently seek stability, sustainability, and security from a product or brand. To drive loyalty, you need to make your customers feel comfortable with your brand at all times. Your customers want to feel like they know what to expect from your brand, and they don't want to be disappointed with a message that runs counter to those expectations.

CLOSEUP

The Three S's of Customer Loyalty

- **Stability:** You emotionally involve your customers when your product or brand sends a consistent message.

- **Sustainability:** You emotionally involve your customers when they know that your product or brand will be with them for a long time or a specific amount of time with a clear end.

- **Security:** You emotionally involve your customers when your product gives them a feeling of comfort or peace-of-mind.

BRANDING CREATES EXPECTATIONS

As you develop your Copywriting Outline, always keep your desired brand image in mind. The consistency used in communicating your brand message will allow customers to feel more confident with it. They will feel more comfortable in trying your product, which will give them the opportunity to personalize it. Your copy should appeal to your target audience's emotional triggers and hype the benefits using language that shows them what's in it for them if they use your product. Once your customers become secure in knowing what they'll get when they buy your product, they're more likely to develop an emotional connection to it and become repeat purchasers.

It's easier and cheaper to keep an existing customer than it is to generate new customers, so don't confuse or disappoint your customers. Let them know what to expect from your brand and deliver on that brand promise every time. That's not to say you can't enhance your brand message, but radically changing it requires a completely new marketing plan in order for the repositioning of your brand to be successful. Think of it this way—imagine you're in a relationship with someone who is a straight-laced, homebody. Then imagine that person shows up for a date with you one night and has done a complete 180-degree turn in terms of his or her appearance, personality or interests. Instead of enjoying watching television and playing Scrabble, this person now wants to get a tattoo of a skeleton on his or her forehead and hit the club scene. How would that make you feel? Most likely, you would be confused and possibly leave the relationship. Branding a product or service works the same way as personal branding in this example.

A sudden change in a brand message (even a personal brand) confuses people and is likely to make them turn away from that brand in search of another that meets their established needs. However, what if the change in brand message was more subtle and occurred over time with minor enhancements along the way? For example, imagine if the person in this relationship slowly began discussing his or her new interests in body art, meeting new people, and trying out some nightclubs. A slow transition, rather than an overnight change, would probably be more acceptable to this person's partner and might result in continued loyalty.

Deliver on your brand promise in every customer interaction.

The same theory holds true for business branding. Customers have expectations for a brand, and once they experience it, they like knowing what they'll get each time they take out their hard-earned money to make a purchase of that brand. Most people are creatures of habit and are adverse to sudden change. A consistent brand message in all forms of business and marketing communications feeds into that habitual nature.

COPYWRITING AND BRANDING RECAP

Remember that consistently communicating your brand message is an essential component to developing your overall image in the marketplace as well as driving customer loyalty and retention. Your copy should not veer too far from the goals of your brand, but first, you need to determine your brand image. This first step is often overlooked but deserves a great deal of time and thought. Your brand image and message is the core of your business. Know your brand image, then make sure the world knows it by offering consistent business and marketing communications.

DESIGN ENHANCES COPY

There are three main components of advertising and each plays an important role in boosting sales:

1. **Placement:** When and where you place your ad
2. **Copywriting:** The words in your ad or marketing piece
3. **Design:** The visual appearance of your ad or marketing piece

When planning your next marketing program, the first step is to define the target audience that you want your message to be seen by and then choose the best medium to place your ad, so that target audience will actually see it. Next, you need to determine the best message for that audience based on your goals for the specific marketing program and then craft the appropriate copy using your Copywriting Outline. Finally, you need to work with a designer to create a visual component to your ad or marketing piece that will enhance your message.

Design can be used in a variety of ways to make your message more compelling. Your designer's role is to help get your message noticed and hold your audience's attention for more than a split second. As you write copy, it's important to create a message flow from your headline to your subhead, key selling points, and call to action. The designer's job is to make sure the audience follows that path through visual cues. (See the Closeup Box for a list of a variety of design techniques that are used in advertising and marketing collateral to increase the effectiveness of the piece.)

Design complements copy.

☀ CLOSEUP

Examples of Design Techniques

- **Text Enhancements:** Typefaces, type sizes, bolding, underlining, italicizing, and capitalization are just a few ways designers can help make certain words and phrases within your copy stand out.

- **Bulleted Lists:** Lists are a great way to call attention to the key selling points and benefits in your copy.

- **Callouts:** A particularly important piece of copy can be highlighted by displaying it separately from the main text of the ad or marketing piece.

- **Sidebars:** Creating an area in your ad or marketing piece that runs down the side of the page to display important copy can be an effective way to draw attention.

- **Pull Quotes:** A specific line of copy used within your ad or marketing piece might be so compelling that it deserves special attention to ensure that the audience sees it. Extracting that line of copy, enclosing it in quotations and setting it off in a larger font than the body of your text can create this effect.

- **Color:** The use of various colors can be extremely effective in drawing customer attention to important copy points.

For example, designers use color and text enhancements like bolding, underlining, capitalization, bulleted lists, etc. to create a roadmap for an audience to follow as they view an ad or marketing piece. However, before you let your designer create the roadmap, make sure you have the path etched out. The design should enhance the copy, not overshadow it. The designer should minimally use each technique to highlight key messages without confusing the audience. Good design will compel your audience to keep reading your ad or marketing piece by showing them where to look next and visually leading them through the marketing messages.

Don't let your designer convince you to give up key elements of your message to work with his or her award-winning design. A good designer will work closely with you to understand the goals of your ad or marketing piece, your brand image, and the specific message you're trying to communicate. Furthermore, a good designer will want to make your copy sing visually rather than play second fiddle to cool visual effects.

The Design and Copy Roadmap: The design of an ad or marketing piece is the visual roadmap, but the copy provides the directions for customers to follow.

CREATING THE HOOK AND REELING THEM IN

Copy and design work closely together to draw in the audience and keep their attention. Words and images work together to hook a customer and reel them in. If the customer resists and starts to lose focus on the ad or marketing piece, another message or graphic should be in place, ready to hook that customer again. This method is repeatedly used in an advertisement or marketing piece to continually hook and reel in your audience until they see the entire message and corresponding call to action.

AVOIDING THE TEXT TRAP

One of the easiest traps to fall into in copywriting is saying too much. Step 7 in the Copywriting Outline (Avoid T.M.I.) discusses this in depth, but it's also important to look at how the K.I.S.S. rule can help the overall design of your ad or marketing piece. The designer's goal is to create a visual path for the audience to follow and receive the copywriter's message. It is difficult for a designer to create a visual path when a page is overflowing with text. Too much copy leaves no room for visual cues. One of the hardest things for copywriters to learn is the importance of white space. Learn to embrace and love white space. It provides visual relief and helps the key selling points of your marketing message to shine through. Use the Red Pen Rule to eliminate extraneous copy and trim your message down to the most powerful points. Not only will your copy have more impact, but your designer will have the required space to make the appearance of your ad stronger. Together, copy and design are an unbeatable team. Don't set them up for failure with an overabundance of words.

chapter sixteen

A Collection of Real-World Small and Medium-Size Business Examples

Nothing helps to explain a theory better than real-world examples. This chapter includes a variety of advertisements, marketing collateral pieces, and website samples from real small and medium-size businesses that will provide tangible examples of copywriting in action. Each example used in this chapter demonstrates a technique or tip that you can use in your Copywriting Outline.

SAMPLE 1
GBW Insurance
Banner Marketing Campground Insurance Programs

GBW Insurance created a banner to market its campground insurance programs. The copy used in the banner provides a great example of how to appeal to an audience's emotional triggers. Using copy that says, "Your business is full of risks. Let *us* work hard to protect *you*." GBW Insurance speaks directly to consumers' emotional triggers of fear, a desire for security, and peace of mind. Words such as *risk* and *protection* further drive the message.

This banner further demonstrates effective copywriting by using the second person and speaking directly to the audience using the words *you* and *your* to personalize the message. The copy is compelling because it's not cluttered with extraneous and meaningless information. Instead, only the most important and actionable information is included. Interestingly, the call to action is also included in GBW Insurance's phone number, 1-800-548-2DAY. This is a clever way to create a call to action.

Your business is full of risks.

Let *us*

work hard

to protect

you.

1-800-548-2DAY

Campground Insurance Programs

SAMPLE 2

GBW Insurance Banner
Marketing Wedding Insurance

GBW Insurance hit a branding home run by using a consistent banner design for marketing its various insurance programs. In this banner example, GBW Insurance is marketing its wedding insurance programs. The layout, color, fonts, and overall design match the company's campground insurance programs banner, creating a unified brand image and consumer message.

Additionally, GBW Insurance continues its use of focused copywriting messages that omit extraneous and meaningless information. The message in the banner is simple, "You've planned for your perfect day. Let us work hard to keep it that way." The copy appeals to the emotional triggers of fear, security, and peace of mind that a person planning a wedding undoubtedly feels, and the copy is written primarily in the second person, which allows the audience to personalize the message. Overall, GBW Insurance has created a compelling marketing campaign with its insurance program banners.

You've planned for your perfect day.

Let *us*
work hard
to keep it
that way.

1-800-548-2DAY

Wedding Insurance

SAMPLE 3

Delatush Systems Direct-Mail Postcard

Delatush Systems created a direct-mail postcard that provides an excellent example of appealing to emotional triggers and writing in the second person. The front of the postcard is effectively written in the active voice and second person and reads, "Reduce your risk. Increase your uptime. Stay compliant." The front of the postcard uses the second person three times and the first person only once. That's a comfortable balance. The copy on the front of the postcard not only speaks directly to the audience, but it also does so while appealing to strong emotional triggers including fear. Finally, the front of the postcard really says it all by including the website address for Delatush Systems. Truth be told, a recipient doesn't even need to look at the back of this postcard to be motivated to act.

The back of this postcard is also well written. A simple list of the main features Delatush Systems offers customers provides the necessary high-level information without harping on extraneous details. The audience learns exactly what's in it for them through the use of strong action-oriented words and phrases including *simplify, automate, reduce costs, save time,* and *eliminate.* Each of the bullets in this list tells the audience W.I.I.F.M. (What's In It For Me) if they do business with Delatush Systems.

Finally, the postcard provides a compelling call to action that includes a special offer that Delatush can easily track, "Would you like to receive 2 free months of Network Monitoring? Give us a call, and we'll tell you how." This call to action is followed by clear instructions on how to contact Delatush Systems for more information including a telephone number, email address, and website, making it extremely easy for recipients to respond. Overall, this postcard hits the mark in terms of its copywriting.

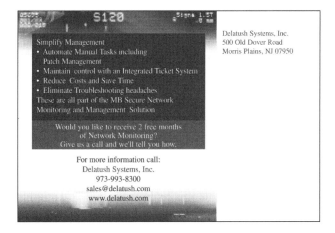

SAMPLE 4

Paisley Enterprises
Booklet Cover

This example demonstrates copywriting for a nontraditional advertising piece. The sample shows the cover of a booklet Paisley Enterprises, a small advertisting and marketing agency, produced for its clients to help them jumpstart their own marketing programs. At the same time, the booklet also worked as a marketing piece for Paisley Enterprises because it demonstrated the agency's knowledge and experience in its field.

The cover copy acts as a headline and encourages recipients to open the booklet to read more from Paisley Enterprises. This copy focuses heavily on using "you" vs. "we" copy and shows the audience exactly W.I.I.F.M. (What's In It For Me) when they read the booklet. In short, the audience will learn to enhance their images and build and grow their businesses. Just fourteen words of copy deliver three strong, personal, and action-oriented messages that work very well together.

SAMPLE 5

Kulture Marketing
Kultivator Newsletter

The Kultivator newsletter from Kulture Marketing provides an excellent example of a business newsletter that is meaningful to customers and clients who receive it. First, the information included in the articles is applicable to the audience and speaks directly to them. Second, the newsletter is predominantly written in the second person. Rather than sounding like a newspaper, the tone is friendlier.

One of the best parts of the Kultivator newsletter is its effective use of expert opinions. (*Note:* Only the front and back of the Kultivator Newletter are included in the example.) The majority of articles in this issue were written by experts in their respective fields. There are many ways to use expert opinions in copywriting to give your business a boost, and Kulture Marketing did just that by taking the time to find experts who provided useful information and tips that spoke directly to the readers of their newsletter.

Kultivator

kulture marketing is a kulture company

Volume 2, Issue 3
September 2007

Demystifying "Coaching"
By Michael Johnson

While most of us have already benefited from coaching in areas including sports, finances and professional or personal life, few know exactly what coaching entails. With its many components and definitions, it is a term that often goes misunderstood.

So what is coaching anyway? How does it work?
Coaching consists of concentrating on the present, identifying what was not working in the past, and focusing on the endless possibility that exists in the future. Coaches begin by asking you, "What do you want to achieve?" From there, they assist you in determining what stands between you and where you want to be. Coaches know the sky is the limit! They are confident that small changes lead to big results. A good coach will empower you to capitalize on your every strength and skill.

He or she won't give advice but will ask the questions that lead you to decide what works best for you.

Good coaches hold you accountable for the goals you set out to achieve. We've all had an experience where we didn't follow through on a plan. Whether because we got sidetracked or hit a challenge along the way, we never attained the intended result. A coach can work beside you as you construct a course of action. He or she will stand by you as you set out to attain your goal. Advice from the right resource can be valuable. However, when it all comes down to it, you are the only one who can decide what you want and how you are going to get it. You are the one who will make steady improvements, who will grow and evolve, and make the changes that turn dreams into reality.

Blogging Promotes Buzz Marketing
A 2007 study conducted by Bridge Ratings and the University of Massachusetts, found that people are most influenced by the opinions of others and word-of-mouth marketing (i.e., friends, family, acquaintances or complete strangers) than any other advertising effort. Blogging is the perfect tool to capitalize on that finding. Blogging promotes two kinds of buzz marketing.

Word-of-mouth marketing: By talking about your blog in all of your business's oral and written communications, you'll generate a verbal buzz.

Viral marketing: By cross-promoting your blog throughout the internet, you'll generate an online buzz.

*For more information on this topic, please see page four: "Blogging Builds Your Brand and Your Business."
by Susan Gunelius*

Special Edition Kultivator:
This special edition is an awesome compilation of articles and tidbits from teacher's, artists, friends and colleagues from around the country. Let's kick off your "school year" with a great plan for your marketing efforts for the remainder of 2007 and a brand new 2008!

Live long and prosper. Leslie

Blogging Builds Your Brand and Business
By Susan Gunelius

Developing an online presence and brand is an essential component of a business's marketing plan. Most companies will launch a website, place some banner ads and search engine ads, send out some direct response emails then wait for the online world to react, visit the website and make a purchase. That kind of passive, reactive marketing doesn't get the job done in the online world anymore.

Instead, marketers must implement more proactive marketing strategies to build their online brand presence and business. One of the least expensive yet most effective ways to do this is by launching a company blog. Blogging has been around for years, and most people think of personal blogs when they hear the term. However, business blogging is growing, and to be a leader in the online market, having a blog is critical.

Successful Content
Don't let your blog fall victim to corporate rhetoric. Your blog has to have something real to say to your readers. It has to connect with your readers. Don't bore them with marketing hype. Be open to criticism and respond to it promptly and respectfully. Make your readers feel like they're welcome and a valuable part of the conversation.

Successful Promotion
Don't think that successful blogging is just a matter of publishing a few posts each week. The key to a powerful blog is consistency. That means consistency in posting, commenting and promoting. Good content will keep readers coming back, and commenting will make them feel like they're part of the conversation. However, one of the most important aspects of developing a successful blog and the brand presence that goes along with it doesn't take place on your blog at all. The time spent cross-promoting it by linking to 100% of his or her time to developing your company's blog as a useful tool. Successful blogging takes an enormous amount of sweat equity but the monetary investment is minimal in comparison to the potential return on that investment.

Establishing a blog is easy and costs virtually nothing, but effectively executing that blog requires commitment. Take your business blog's role in your overall marketing plan seriously by hiring a professional with extensive blogging and social media experience who can dedicate 100% of his or her time to developing your company's blog as a useful tool. Successful blogging takes an enormous amount of sweat equity but the monetary investment is minimal in comparison to the potential return on that investment.

Blogging generates word-of-mouth advertising through the immense social networking infrastructure of the online community.

and commenting on other sites and blogs as well as participating in relevant user forums and social networks like Digg.com, StumbleUpon.com and Reddit.com are crucial components to your blog's success.

Susan Gunelius spent over a decade managing marketing programs for Fortune 500 companies.

Currently, she is a freelance writer and the author of two popular marketing blogs at www.MarketingBurb.com and www.BrandFoew.com

A Company Blog Can Directly Affect Your Bottom-Line:

■ Blogging generates word-of-mouth advertising through the immense social networking infrastructure of the online community.

■ Blogging converts readers into customers. When visitors read your blog, they can be moved to action through compelling content.

■ Blogging helps existing customers feel like they're part of a community and like their opinions are heard through the blog's use of comments and follow up.

■ Simply stated, blogs establish a connection with people and therefore a connection to your business. However, that connection needs to be perceived as a personal one. The value of the connection created at your company blog will grow through relevant content and consistent promotion.

> Education's purpose is to replace an empty mind with an open one.
>
> –Malcon Forbes

4.

Kultivator is published by Kulture Marketing.
for a complimentary subscription or to add a friend to our mailing list,
please e-mail Kulture Marketing at mailer@kulturemarketing.com

Kulture Marketing • 230 Passaic Avenue • Fairfield, NJ 07004   973 276 9400 · fax 973-276-9411 · www.kulturemarketing.com

(continued on pg. 3)

SAMPLE 6

The Etiquette & Protocol School
Website

The Etiquette & Protocol School has a very professional website. However, that level of professionalism doesn't mean there isn't room for a conversational tone in the company's copywriting. This page from The Etiquette & Protocol School's website provides a great example of copywriting that effectively uses questions to create a conversational tone and draws the audience into the dialogue. Take note of the first paragraph under the "CEO Training" heading; it provides a series of questions directed at the reader using the second person. The questions not only engage the reader, but they also appeal to the reader's emotional triggers of fear and a desire to be a leader.

The Etiquette & Protocol School

Business Etiquette Intelligence Reformation

| Business Etiquette & Professional Enrichment Programs | Customer Service Training | CEO Training & International Protocol | Children, Teen & Young Adult Programs | Special Event Programs |

Irene A. Founder | Philosophy

"If there is any one secret of success, it lies in the ability to get the other person's point of view and see things from his angle as well as your own."

—Henry Ford

Etiquette Answers
to Your Questions

CEO Training

Are you on your way to the top of the corporate ladder and you are wondering if you missed any steps along the way? You know you have the intelligence and the skills required to be a CEO, however, do you have the grace, social skills, and invisible knowledge mandatory to truly be a "success story?"

Business Etiquette Intelligence is not an option for doing business in the global corporate arena, it is a necessity.

The CEO Training is singularly designed for each professional and tailored to his or her specific needs.

Topics include but are not limited to:

- Handshaking
- Eye Contact
- Introducing Yourself and Others
- Conversation Skills
- Power Projection
- Dining Like a Diplomat
- Cost-Effective Entertaining
- Managing Different Personalities
- Your Business Style
- International Business Skills

International Protocol

A cultural faux pas in the business arena may have serious and resounding consequences. Because corporate America thrives within a global economy, it is important for businesses to be keenly aware of international cultural differences.

We offer culturally specific presentations for corporations, universities, and travel organizations to prepare them for a successful international experience.

Topics covered may include:

- Corporate Protocol
- Languages
- Dress Codes
- Forms of Address
- Greetings
- Social Situations
- Dining Do's & Don'ts
- Tipping
- Gift Giving

Home | Contact Us

SAMPLE 7

Paisley Enterprises
Valentine's Day CD Giveaway—Promotional Item

Paisley Enterprises Valentine's Day CD cover represents another way copy can be used in nontradiional advertising. Even a gift to customers or clients can become a marketing opportunity with the use of effective copy. Paisley Enterprises used a friendly tone in a note to recipients placed inside the cover of the company's Valentine's Day CD gift. The fun tone is appropriate for the piece and the occasion.

Additionally, the use of the abbreviated, "U R GR8!" instead of the full words, "You are great!" demonstrates how incorrect spelling can be acceptable when it matches the tone of the piece and doesn't detract from the overall message. The tagline of the note provides another example of effective copy, "Celebrating 10 years of making you look good," which cleverly promotes the company's 10-year anniversary with personalized language written in the second person.

Be Ours, Valentine!

WE'RE SPREADING SOME PAISLEY LOVE IN HONOR OF OUR
FAVORITE HOLIDAY AND ITS CHUBBY CHERUBIC MESSENGER CUPID.
WHETHER YOU'RE A BRAND NEW CLIENT OR AN OLE' FAITHFUL,
WE WANT YOU TO KNOW WE'RE GLAD YOU'RE OUR YEAR-ROUND
VALENTINE, WE APPRECIATE YOUR BUSINESS AND, U R GR8!

ENJOY THE ENCLOSED *Paisley Love* CD FILLED WITH
NOTHING BUT LOVE SONGS...HAPPY VALENTINE'S DAY!

PAISLEYINC.COM
973 276 9400

CELEBRATING 10 YEARS OF MAKING YOU LOOK GOOD.

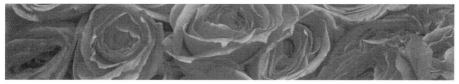

SAMPLE 8

Somerset Home for Temporarily Displaced Children
2005 Annual Report

The annual report from Somerset Home for Temporarily Displaced Children provides a relevant example of how copywriting is important even in nontraditional communications such as an annual report. Most annual reports begin with a letter from the organization's leader, and Somerset Home's annual report does not deviate from this format. However, instead of using a letter that simply touts the organization's many accomplishments over the course of the prior year, the letter from the executive director speaks directly to readers as "you" and uses a very conversational tone. Readers are immediately drawn into the conversation and encouraged to continue reading. While many annual reports are full of dry, corporate rhetoric, the Somerset Home annual report invites readers to get involved and makes the information contained within the report more meaningful.

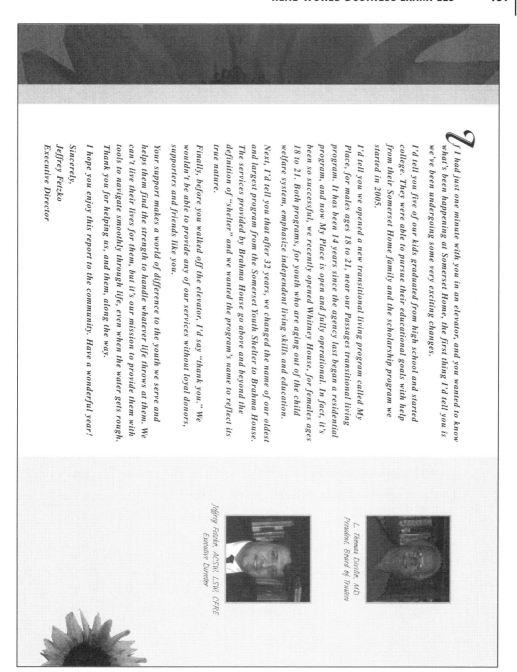

If I had just one minute with you in an elevator, and you wanted to know what's been happening at Somerset Home, the first thing I'd tell you is we've been undergoing some very exciting changes.

I'd tell you five of our kids graduated from high school and started college. They were able to pursue their educational goals with help from their Somerset Home family and the scholarship program we started in 2005.

I'd tell you we opened a new transitional living program called My Place, for males ages 18 to 21, near our Passages transitional living program. It has been 14 years since the agency last began a residential program, and now My Place is open and fully operational. In fact, it's been so successful, we recently opened Whitney House, for females ages 18 to 21. Both programs, for youth who are aging out of the child welfare system, emphasize independent living skills and education.

Next, I'd tell you that after 32 years, we changed the name of our oldest and largest program from the Somerset Youth Shelter to Brahma House. The services provided by Brahma House go above and beyond the definition of "shelter" and we wanted the program's name to reflect its true nature.

Finally, before you walked off the elevator, I'd say "thank you." We wouldn't be able to provide any of our services without loyal donors, supporters and friends like you.

Your support makes a world of difference to the youth we serve and helps them find the strength to handle whatever life throws at them. We can't live their lives for them, but it's our mission to provide them with tools to navigate smoothly through life, even when the water gets rough. Thank you for helping us, and them, along the way.

I hope you enjoy this report to the community. Have a wonderful year!

Sincerely,
Jeffrey Fetzko
Executive Director

Jeffrey Fetzko, ACSW, LSW, CFRE
Executive Director

L. Thomas Davide, MD
President, Board of Trustees

SAMPLE 9

Paisley Enterprises
Newsletter

Paisley Enterprises clearly made a conscious effort with its Paisley Ink newsletter to create a conversational and fun tone. The copy focuses heavily on the second person in a highly inviting style that includes simple writing and intentional grammatical errors (sentence fragments) to match the fun tone. The bulk of the newsletter includes useful, W.I.I.F.M. articles with company information taking a secondary position in terms of importance. The tone creates a sense of family and demonstrates how copy used in a newsletter can be far less "salesy" than copy used in an advertisement or brochure.

VOLUME 4/ISSUE 2 • WWW.PAISLEYINC.COM • 973 403 0912 • FAX 973 403 0484 • 2ND QUARTER 2002

Web Sites that Work

The Internet is a vast world of click-here's and click-there's and can be a confusing and okay, sometimes annoying, adventure! We've all been down the techno-road of slow load times, the unprintable page of text and hmmm...did that order go through on my credit card or not.

The good news is you can offer your customers an informative and fun website that works efficiently...if you plan ahead!

Map It Out

The Golden Rule of web design! Before you think about what colors your site should have or what photos you're going to use, you must map out your website. Think content — how many pages do you need and what info will be on each page? To help you, consider two things: 1) What information or messages do you want your client to know about you (your history, a staff list, your mission statement), and 2) What information does your client want from you (your product line, how to order, contact info)?

Happy Home Page

This is where the first impression comes in. For a spectacular intro to that loyal client or hot prospect...keep it simple! Your home page design should have three goals: 1) to create a great first impression, 2) to act as a table of contents for the site, and 3) to give a BRIEF overview (let's say a paragraph or two at the most) of who you are and what you do.

User-Friendly Navigation

Don't leave your customer lost in cyberspace.

www.medtile.com

www.njcoeac.org

www.paisleyinc.com

Your mission is to enable your visitors to enter your site quickly, locate the content options within a nano-second and with a simple click, get to the section of their choice. Make sure you have the same table of contents on every page and if you link to another site, make it easy to return to yours. In general, don't load up your site with too many links — you want to be a helpful reference, but you also want them to stay on your site! Also, too many subcategories can be unnerving, so be careful to organize your content in a user-friendly manner. Remember: you know all there is to know

about your company and more, but your clients don't necessarily need to know every last detail — at least not through your web site.

Copy & Long Scrolling Pages

Statistics show that most people prefer to do as little scrolling as possible. For that reason, make sure all critical content and navigation options are on the tops of your pages or along the sides. Spare your clients from long scrolls — the less work they have to do, the better!

Sometimes, however, scrolling is unavoidable in your line of business because of the extent of content you may need to present. Either way, a good rule of thumb is to try and keep your copy as concise and to the point as possible.

Bells & Whistles vs. Load Time

Admittedly, there are some super cool animations, mpegs and intros that can be created for web sites. But, there are plenty of people still surfing on dial-up and even if a visitor has the fastest of DSLs, no one wants to wait while your super cool movie downloads. You run the risk of losing more traffic because you've loaded your home page or subsequent pages with images that are too large or too involved to download quickly. Bells & whistles can enhance your site and are interesting to watch, but for the most part, the Internet is moving toward a trend of simplicity. People want to find the info they are seeking quickly.

If you'd like to refresh your web site or create a new one, give us a call at 973.403.0912 — we'd love to help! ✂

Paisley Team Update

Leslie List, President, has been appointed Vice President, Marketing of the Essex County Chapter of New Jersey Women's Business Owners Association (NJAWBO). She will coordinate the marketing efforts for the organization including its quarterly newsletter and calendar of events, beginning in July.

Etta Jane Pagani has returned for her fourth consecutive summer internship. Etta will be entering her junior year at The George Washington University — time sure flies — and she'll be with us until the end of August. Her year away included a full class schedule and a new position as Business Manager for GWBlitz!, an on-line & print news magazine on campus.

Laura Schmude joined us as Senior Art Director in January, having relocated from Brooklyn to New Jersey. A graduate of UCLA, Laura's career has included design and production in the in-house marketing department of Goldman Sachs and web design for NYC agency, Clik Communications. Originally from Ohio, Laura is now an integral part of our team adding her expertise in web design and PowerPoint presentations. One of her first projects here was to re-design our website. Check it out at www.paisleyinc.com!

Gail P. Stone, Vice President of Marketing, has recently been appointed Executive Vice President of the North Essex Chamber of Commerce. The Chamber, formerly the West Essex Chamber, completed a successful merger with the Montclair Chamber in January 2002 and now encompasses nine Essex County towns. The new position also means that Gail is the President-Elect for the organization beginning her term in July 2003.

Gail has also been elected Secretary on the Board of Directors of Habitat for Humanity Newark and begins her second year as a Trustee. The nonprofit organization builds homes for those in need in the Central Ward of Newark, NJ. ✂

(L to R: Leslie List, Gail P. Stone and Laura Schmude)

LESSONS TO LEARN

As you review the real-world samples in this chapter and throughout this book, consider how you can use the same tactics to help boost copywriting for your own business. Doing this type of research is critical to developing your skills as a copywriter. Follow your Copywriting Outline and remember to update it as you find new ideas, concepts, and examples that you can leverage. Remember, the Copywriting Outline is a working document. It is most valuable when you continuously work to improve it and make it as comprehensive as you can.

chapter seventeen

Samples and Practical Examples

The Copywriting Outlines used in this chapter provide some high-level examples of the information you can use to create copy for advertising and marketing campaigns for your target audience. It is important to analyze your business, customers, and competition thoroughly to complete the most in-depth Copywriting Outline possible. Remember, the Copywriting Outline is an ever-evolving document. The more details you include in your Copywriting Outline, the better your copy will be for future marketing and advertising initiatives.

Additionally, the advertising and marketing examples in this chapter demonstrate how you can use your Copywriting Outline to create copy for various media. Each example uses a simple design rather than visual imagery to highlight the copy. You'll notice these examples communicate a consistent message and design to deliver a strong brand image. One of the most important learning points to take away from these examples is the way that you can repeatedly use key messages from the

Copywriting Outline to consistently communicate your key selling points and brand to your target audience. These materials should work together to drive awareness, recognition, and ultimately, sales and referrals.

CONSOLIDATED COPYWRITING OUTLINE: ABC TAX SERVICES

Product or Service Name or Target Audience

Federal income tax return preparation for taxpayers expecting a refund. (*Note:* Other target audiences include taxpayers expecting to have a balance due on their tax returns, customers with individual taxpayer returns, customers with business returns, etc., and each audience should have a separate Copywriting Outline dedicated to them.)

Step 1: Exploit Your Product's Benefits—How is my product better than other similar products available (i.e., the competition)? Why is my product the best?

- **Feature:** Trained tax preparers
  - **Benefit:** With our tax preparers, errors are less likely to appear on your return. You'll have peace of mind that your return will be processed smoothly and your refund will arrive quickly. Emotional triggers = trust and instant gratification.
  - **Benefit:** We'll find every deduction to maximize your refund. Emotional trigger = desire to get a good deal.
- **Feature:** Provide e-file services
  - **Benefit:** You'll get your refund fast because your return will be immediately sent to the IRS, rather than in days or weeks by snail mail. Emotional trigger = instant gratification.

- **Feature:** Ten member staff with six tax preparers, one computer technician, two receptionists, and one mail clerk
  - **Benefit:** Our large staff means your business and questions will be addressed quickly; however, we are small enough to know who you are when you call. You get one-on-one, personal service every time you stop by or call, and you're treated like our top priority. Emotional triggers = instant gratification.
- **Feature:** Provide audit protection service
  - **Benefit:** If your return is flagged for an audit, one of our tax preparers will help you navigate through the communications with the IRS until the audit is over. Emotional trigger = trust.

Step 2: Exploit Your Competition's Weaknesses—How are my competitors' products inferior to mine?

- They offer no peace-of-mind guarantee. ABC Tax Services provides a Confidence Guarantee that no other tax preparer can beat. If you receive a refund that is different from what ABC Tax Services quotes, ABC Tax Services will refund the difference (up to 10%, excluding withholdings for IRS or medical debt or other liens against the refund). *Notice how the guarantee was branded as a Confidence Guarantee to further appeal to consumers' desire for trust and security.*
- They employ tax preparers who are not members of the National Association of Tax Practitioners. You can rest assured that your tax return will be prepared accurately because every tax preparer at ABC Tax Services has passed stringent testing requirements set by the National Association of Tax Practitioners. That's just one more way ABC Tax Services helps you safely navigate the tax maze.

- They offer no audit assistance. If your tax return is flagged for audit, you won't be left alone. A representative from ABC Tax Services will work with you to navigate the audit process from start to finish.
- They charge for e-filing. ABC Tax Services will e-file your tax return for free, so you'll get your refund fast at no extra charge.
- They don't have a live answering service. ABC Tax Services is here when you need help. A representative answers our phones 24 hours per day, which means you can call us any time you need us. Don't wait until tomorrow morning. Call now!

Step 3: Know Your Audience—Who should buy my product or who is likely to want or need it (i.e., target audience/market)? Who will see my ad?

- Target Audience: Taxpayers expecting a refund
  - Common demographics of target audience:
    - Married
    - Children under 18 years of age
    - Homeowner
    - Age 25–45
    - Income between $30,000–75,000
    - Interests include family activities such as sports, travel, movies, dining out

Step 4: Communicate W.I.F.M. (What's In It For Me?)—How can I elaborate on my product's benefits and differentiators to tell customers specifically how the product will positively affect their lives?

- Get money in your pocket *fast* with e-filing.
- You can put *more* money in your wallet because ABC Tax Services finds even the smallest deductions.

- Save money with *free* e-filing.
- Reduce the stress of tax time. Let the professionals at ABC Tax Services do the work for you.
- Never worry about an audit again. ABC Tax Services' audit protection service will help you if your return is flagged for audit by the IRS.

Step 5: Focus on "You," Not "We"—How can I word my product's benefits and differentiators so they talk *to* the customer and not *about* me?

- What do you want to spend your tax refund on this year? Pay down some bills? Go on vacation? Whatever you want to do with that money, you can do it faster with ABC Tax Services' free e-filing program.
- You've already waited long enough for your tax refund. Don't wait any longer.
- Tax time stressing you out? You deserve some peace of mind. Call ABC Tax Services and forget about those worries.

Step 6: Know Your Medium—Where will I be advertising? How can I write copy to maximize the space provided by that medium?

- Placing an ad in the local newspaper's lifestyles section where the target audience is likely to see it. Benefits to focus on:
  - Fast refund
  - Maximum refund
  - Free e-filing

Step 7: Avoid T.M.I. (Too Much Information)—What information is important to me but not helpful in an ad (i.e., may be useful in a news article or brochure in the future)? How can I keep my ad copy from becoming cluttered?

- Examples of jargon to avoid:
  - Practitioner
- Elements that can be omitted from a newspaper ad to taxpayers expecting a refund (limited space for key messages):
  - Audit protection
  - Confidence Guarantee
  - Staffing

Step 8: Include a Call to Action—What is my call to action? What do I want my customers to do as soon as they read my ad? How can I create a sense of urgency?

- Call now.
- Stop by today.
- April 15th is almost here.
- Don't delay.
- It's tax time already.
- The IRS is waiting for your return.
- The clock is ticking.
- Get your refund fast.
- You've already waited long enough for that money.
- Don't wait any longer for your refund.

Step 9: C.Y.A. (Cover Your Ass)—What are some phrases I want to remember to include in my ads to protect myself? Is there anything else I need to remember to back up my claims?

- **Confidence Guarantee:** Up to 10%, excluding withholdings for IRS or medical debt or other liens against the refund.
- **Audit protection:** For a maximum of one year from the date of first contact regarding the audit from the IRS, a representative will be available via telephone for consultation and will attend one face-to-face meeting with the IRS (taxpayer responsible for travel expenses).

Step 10: Proofread—Who can proofread my ad for me? What tools are available to help me proofread my ad?

- Employees
- Spell check
- Dictionary
- Attorney

ADVERTISING AND MARKETING EXAMPLES FROM ABC TAX SERVICES

The key selling point for the target audience of taxpayers expecting a refund on their tax returns is ABC Tax Services' ability to deliver those refunds quickly through their free e-filing service. ABC Tax Services also wants to promote the ability of their preparers to find even the smallest deductions thereby maximizing refund amounts. Additionally, ABC Tax Services feels their target audience of taxpayers expecting a refund will be interested in their Customer Confidence Guarantee and their audit protection program, which helps customers feel like they are in good hands when they choose ABC Tax Services.

EXAMPLE 1

Newspaper Print Ad

ABC Tax Services has budgeted for a small ad in the local newspaper, which means there won't be a lot of space to communicate a variety of messages. With that in mind, the ABC Tax Services' headline needs to focus on the strongest message that will SLAP the target audience. ABC Tax Services chose to **S**top customers with their fast refunds message. The copy draws the reader in further (**L**ook) by appealing to an emotional trigger of instant gratification and telling the reader they've already waited long enough for their tax refund. The ad wraps up with a strong call to action (**A**ct) and contact information that is intended to lead to a **P**urchase. Notice that the use of white space provides visual relief from the commonly text-heavy pages of a newspaper. Together, the copy and simple design maximize the small space that the newspaper ad provides.

EXAMPLE 2

Flyer

A flyer is a take-away item. It's meant to catch a customer's attention and provide some details about a business' key selling points or special offers. ABC Tax Services uses this flyer to highlight its key selling points, but instead of simply listing features, the copy first focuses on emotional triggers and benefits and then on features.

The flyer starts with a strong hook—fast refunds equal instant gratification by immediately putting money in the customer's pocket. Additional information is included under the headline to further clarify it and reinforce the main message and benefits to customers. Next, the key selling points list benefits in bold type, and emotional triggers act as lead-ins for each bullet. If customers simply scan the flyer, they see the headline and bolded text in the list. This should be enough to interest the target audience and get them to read further. The flyer provides significantly more of ABC Tax Services' story than a small newspaper ad provides. Finally, the ad closes with a call to action, contact information, and a disclaimer to protect ABC Tax Services.

Get Your Tax Refund Fast and Use That Money Now!

**You've waited long enough for your tax refund.
Don't wait another day!**

**Call ABC Tax Services today
and get your refund fast with FREE e-filing.**

You'll enjoy these benefits when you choose ABC Tax Services:

√ **Fast refunds:** ABC Tax Services will e-file your return for FREE! Not only will you get your refund fast, but you'll also save money with free e-filing.

√ **Big refunds:** You'll get the largest tax refund possible because ABC Tax Services will take the time to find even the smallest deductions for you.

√ **Service you can trust:** You can rest assured your tax return will be prepared accurately because all of the tax preparers at ABC Tax Services have passed stringent certification exams. That's just one more way you can feel safe working with ABC Tax Services.

√ **Service when you need it:** You need help at tax time, and ABC Tax Services is available 24-hours per day through our special customer hotline to help you with any questions or problems you may have.

√ **Peace-of-mind:** Leave the stress of tax time to the pros at ABC Tax Services through our Customer Confidence Guarantee. If you receive a refund different from what our preparers quote, ABC Tax Services will refund the difference directly to you.*

Call 222-555-1111 now and start using your refund.

222-555-1111   444 Main St.   Smithtown   www.abctaxs.com
Conveniently located in the Wal-Mart shopping center

Refunds available up to 10% of quoted refund amount excluding withholdings for IRS or medical debt or other liens against the refund.

EXAMPLE 3

Business Card

A business card is often thought of simply as an informational tool, but it's another monetary investment that can be turned into a marketing opportunity. The business card for ABC Tax Services provides the information a customer expects to see, but it also includes five key selling points for customers. The company paid for the space, and they're using it to their advantage.

ABC Tax Services
444 Main Street
Smithtown, XX 00000
www.abctaxs.com

Jane Doe
Tax Professional

Phone: 222-555-1111
Fax: 222-555-3333
Email: jdoe@abctaxs.com

√ Professional tax service
√ Fast refunds
√ Free e-filing
√ Confidence Guarantee
√ Audit protection

EXAMPLE 4

Point-of-Sale Counter Card

A point-of-sale counter card is a marketing piece that typically sits on the desk or counter where a purchase is made. In ABC Tax Services' office, the counter card sits on the preparer's desk, so customers can see it while the preparer is working on their returns. The headline focuses on the key selling point for taxpayers expecting a refund, and the copy goes on to appeal to the emotional trigger of instant gratification. Finally, the call to action is specific to the exact moment of the purchase decision with copy that says, "Ask how."

Get Your Refund FAST!

Don't wait any longer than you already have for your refund.

Ask how you can get your refund fast at no extra charge.

ABC TAX

EXAMPLE 5

Banner

A banner works similarly to an outdoor billboard advertisement. It's meant to catch the attention of passersby, pique their interest, and generate awareness for a business or product. With that in mind, the copy for ABC Tax Services' banner is extremely simple and focuses on the key selling point for the target audience. Words that will help **S**top the audience as part of the SLAP technique are set in a bold and large font, which draws attention and delivers the key message even faster than a complete sentence.

EXAMPLE 6
Direct-Mail Postcard

A direct-mail piece provides more information than many other types of advertising simply because there is more space with which to work. However, don't fall into the trap of overloading that space with copy. Choose the most compelling messages for the target audience and adhere to the K.I.S.S. rule. Providing too much information will confuse the recipient and likely relegate your expensive mail piece to the garbage can. While it can be tempting to write a lengthy letter, consider the audience and your message before you compose your copy. A two-page letter probably will be far less effective than a well-written and well-designed one-page note.

The postcard for ABC Tax Services focuses on the key selling point on the front with no extraneous details. There is no doubt what message the recipient is meant to understand when they pull this postcard out of the mailbox. The back of the postcard reiterates the key selling point and appeals to the emotional trigger of instant gratification.

This example shows how the call to action can effectively appear before the benefits in an ad or marketing piece. This technique is useful in creating a strong sense of urgency. Perhaps this postcard will be mailed during the latter half of the tax season when the clock is ticking and customers simply need to find someone to help them file their tax returns on time. The call to action up-front is more effective in a situation such as this when customers are in buying mode and just need help or direction. At this point in time, the additional benefits and selling points might not be as important to customers as the phone number of someone who can help them immediately.

Get Your Tax Refund FAST

You've waited long enough for your tax refund. Don't wait another day!

Call ABC Tax Services today at
222-555-1111
and ask to get your refund fast with free e-filing.

√ **Get money in your pocket fast.**

√ **Put more money back in your wallet** when ABC Tax Services finds every possible deduction.

√ **Save money** with free e-filing.

√ **Reduce the stress of tax time** by letting ABC Tax Services do the work for you.

ABC Tax Services
444 Main St.
Smithtown (in the Wal-Mart shopping center)
www.abctaxs.com

ABC TAX

John Doe
123 Main St.
Smithtown, ZZ 00000

CONSOLIDATED COPYWRITING OUTLINE: ONCE AGAIN CHILDREN'S CONSIGNMENTS

Product or Service Name or Target Audience

Merchandise for expectant or new mothers looking to purchase items for their babies. (*Note:* Other target audiences could include mothers of older children, consignors who sell merchandise, etc., and each audience should have a separate Copywriting Outline dedicated to it.)

Step 1: Exploit Your Product's Benefits—How is my product better than other similar products available (i.e., the competition)? Why is my product the best?

- **Feature:** Low prices
    - **Benefit:** Save money, cheaper than buying new—helps customers save money at a time when expenses are high. Why pay full price? Emotional trigger = desire for a good value.
- **Feature:** High quality
    - **Benefit:** Items look as good as new and are reviewed for quality before being sold (Good-As-New Test)—helps customers feel better about buying used merchandise for their babies. Emotional triggers = feelings of guilt and fear.
- **Feature:** 2,500 square-foot store
    - **Benefit:** Large store means wide variety of merchandise. Save time with one-stop shopping. Emotional trigger = desire for more free time.

Step 2: Exploit Your Competition's Weaknesses—How are my competitors' products inferior to mine?

- **Lower quality:** They don't use a "Good-As-New Test" and accept any item (junk).
- **Less convenient location:** We're located in the shopping center next to a popular grocery store, FoodMart; the competitor is located five miles out of town.
- **Hours:** We're open Saturdays and Sundays. The competitor is not open on Sundays.
- **Delivery:** We deliver oversized items. The competitor does not.
- **Return policy:** We accept returns within one week. The competitor does not accept returns.

Step 3: Know Your Audience—Who should buy my product or who is likely to want or need it (i.e., target audience/market)? Who will see my ad?

- **Target audience:** New mothers and expectant mothers
  - Common demographics of target audience
    - Age 25–35
    - Married
    - Young children under 3 years old
    - Income $20,000–70,000 per year
    - Belong to local parenting or mother groups
    - Read parenting magazines
    - Internet users
    - Coupon users

Step 4: Communicate W.I.I.F.M. (What's In It For Me?)—How can I elaborate on my product benefits and differentiators to tell customers specifically how the product will affect their lives in a positive manner?

- **Save money:** Use the money you save for other things.
- **You're busy:** Don't spend your time driving around town.
- **Quality:** Get as good as new for a lot less money. Why spend full price?
- **Don't settle for less than the best:** Just because it's used doesn't mean it shouldn't be top quality. Consignment doesn't mean junk. You deserve good as new.

Step 5: Focus on "You," Not "We"—How can I word my product's benefits and differentiators so they talk *to* the customer and not *about* me?

- When you shop at Once Again Children's Consignments you can use the money you save for other things like paying bills or having fun with your family!
- Shopping for a new baby can be expensive, but you can save up to 90% without sacrificing quality when you shop at Once Again Children's Consignments.
- Your baby deserves the best. Once Again Children's Consignments puts each item sold at our store through a stringent Good-As-New Test. Everything you buy at our store is as good as new but costs a lot less.
- A new baby = a busy mom! You can shop at Once Again Children's Consignments seven days per week for a full selection of baby products at prices you can afford. We're conveniently located next to the FoodMart. Baby shopping just got a lot easier!

Step 6: Know Your Medium—Where will I be advertising? How can I write copy to maximize the space provided by that medium?

- Placing an ad in the local newspaper's lifestyle section where the target audience is likely to see it. Benefits focus on:
    - Low prices
    - High quality
    - Wide selection

Step 7: Avoid T.M.I. (Too Much Information)—What information is important to me but not helpful in an ad (i.e., may be useful in a news article or brochure in the future)? How can I keep my ad copy from becoming cluttered?

- Elements that can be omitted from a newspaper ad due to limited space for key messages:
    - Delivery
    - Store space
    - Return policy

Step 8: Include a Call to Action—What is my call to action? What do I want my customers to do as soon as they read my ad? How can I create a sense of urgency?

- Stop by today
- Don't wait any longer to save money

- Visit today
- Don't miss it
- While supplies last
- For a limited time only
- Call now
- Hurry in

Step 9: C.Y.A. (Cover Your Ass)—What are some phrases I want to remember to include in my ads to protect myself? Is there anything else I need to remember to back up my claims?

- **Sold as is:** All merchandise is sold as is in used condition.
- **Prices final:** All prices are final.
- **Delivery:** Delivery available within 20-mile radius of store for items marked "Delivery available" on the price tag. Deliveries made within seven days of purchase.
- **Returns:** Merchandise may be returned within seven days of purchase with receipt.

Step 10: Proofread—Who can proofread my ad for me? What tools are available to help me proofread my ad?

- Family
- Friends
- Spell check
- Dictionary

ADVERTISING AND MARKETING EXAMPLES FOR ONCE AGAIN CHILDREN'S CONSIGNMENTS

The key selling point for the target audience of expectant and new mothers is Once Again Children's Consignments' low prices. Part of that key selling point is a quality commitment. Additionally, the target audience benefits from the store's convenient location and hours. These are the copy points Once Again Children's Consignments will communicate in its various advertisements and marketing materials that are targeted to expectant and new mothers.

EXAMPLE 1

Newspaper Ad

Once Again Children's Consignments has a small advertising budget and decides to place an ad in the local section of the newspaper. The headline grabs the attention of frugal mothers by focusing on low prices and top quality. With limited space available, Once Again Children's Consignments decides to focus on quantifiable differentiators by citing its "up to 90%" savings offer and its "good-as-new" commitment. These messages should interest the target audience who may not be familiar with Once Again Children's Consignments quality program.

EXAMPLE 2

Flyer

As you know, a flyer has more space for copy. A flyer should grab the audience's attention with a targeted headline (in this case, Once Again Children's Consignments focuses on low prices and convenience). Then quantify and clarify those benefits. Once Again Children's Consignments does this using a numbered list in a callout box. The callout provides an ordered list of the most important benefits to the target audience and then leads into the call to action. A sense of urgency is created by tying the message directly to customers' needs.

Once Again Children's Consignments

Expect the best for less!

Don't waste time and money.
Shop at Once Again Children's Consignments
for all your baby's needs.

The Once Again Commitment to You:

1. You can **save up to 90%***

2. You'll get the best quality thanks to our
Good-As-New Quality Test
(only the best items are sold at Once Again Children's Consignments).

3. You'll **save time** because
everything you need for your baby can be found
at Once Again Children's Consignments.

Baby shopping has never been easier on your wallet or your schedule!

Convenient Location:	999 West St. in Smithville (Next to the FoodMart). Call us at 222-555-9999 for directions.
Convenient Hours:	Open 7 days per week from 10:00 a.m. to 6:00 p.m.

Stop by today
before the best seasonal items and deals are gone!

*Savings based on suggested retail price for new merchandise.

EXAMPLE 3

Direct Mail

Once Again Children's Consignments starts its direct-mail letter with a bang. The headline speaks directly to the recipient and focuses on emotional triggers to which a new mother would respond. Once Again Children's Consignments personalizes the letter in the greeting, which tremendously helps its effectiveness. Nothing says, "Throw me in the garbage can," more than an anonymously addressed letter (think Dear Sir or To Resident). The copy is further connected to the individual receiving it by citing a current event in the recipient's life (birth of a baby). The copy also personalizes the business and connects it to the customer by saying the owners of the consignment shop are mothers, too. This creates a subconscious camaraderie and a feeling of, "I'll feel comfortable and welcome if I shop at Once Again Children's Consignments."

Now that the letter has effectively reached out to the recipient, the benefits of shopping at Once Again Children's Consignments are listed, followed by a call to action and a tracking mechanism. A postscript is a useful tool to draw attention to a final message. The postscript used in the letter creates a sense of urgency around the call to action. The messages are laid out well and create a path for the customer to follow. There will be customers who choose not to read an entire letter. For those customers, bold faced type and boxed callouts are used to draw attention to the most important messages. Even if the customer doesn't read the entire letter, the attention-grabbing bold type ensures that the customer will have enough information to act.

It's also important to point out that teaser copy could be included on the envelope. For example, "Save up to 90% on all your baby needs. Learn how inside," could be an effective way to use copy to lure customers into opening, rather than tossing, your direct-mail piece. Of course, an asterisk and any necessary disclaimers need to be included with this specific claim.

**Top-quality Baby Items at Prices You Can Afford.
Shopping for Your Baby Just Got Easier.**

999 West St.
Smithville, XX 99999
(222) 555-9999
jdoe@onceagainchildrens.com

November 1, 2008

Dear Ms. Smith:

Congratulations on your new bundle of joy! Welcoming a baby into the world is a busy time for most mothers with one expense after another. That's why Once Again Children's Consignments focuses on delivering a **full line of top-quality baby products at the lowest possible prices**.

We're mothers, too, and we know what it's like. We're here to help you get through the child-rearing years without breaking the bank.

When you shop at Once Again Children's Consignments, you will:

➢ **Save Money:** You can feel confident you're getting the best price for every item. Use the money you save for other things like paying bills or splurging on a dinner out or a fun family activity.

➢ **Get Top Quality:** Why pay full price when you can get *as good-as-new* merchandise for a lot less money? Every item sold at Once Again Children's Consignments passes a stringent Good-As-New Quality Test. Unlike some consignment stores, you won't find junk (or less than the best) at Once Again Consignments.

➢ **Enjoy Convenience:** New moms are busy. That's why Once Again Children's Consignments carries a wide selection of baby and children's products. From clothing to strollers, toys and everything in between, you'll find it here at the best prices. To make it even easier for you to do your baby shopping, we're located next to the FoodMart and open everyday from 10:00 a.m. until 6:00 p.m. It's never been easier or more economical to shop for your little one.

Don't waste time and money. Stop by Once Again Children's Consignments today for all your baby's needs. Your wallet will thank you, and your baby will get the best for less.

> **Bring this letter to get 10% off a single purchase made before December 15, 2008.**

All the best,

Jane Doe

Jane Doe
Owner

P.S. Our winter seasonal merchandise is now available. Hurry in while supplies last!

EXAMPLE 4
Coupon

The offer is the most important part of a coupon. It either is used to encourage new customers to make their first purchase or entice existing customers to purchase again. Coupons may not be the best strategy for every business since the business will need to lose a bit of profit on each redeemed coupon, but to generate new customers, Once Again Children's Consignments decided to pass out coupons at the FoodMart adjacent to their store. Notice that the coupon is uncluttered, easy to see, and includes only a headline, the offer, disclaimers, and the business' logo. The offer, along with a well-written headline, draws the customer in and encourages them to take a further look. Next, if space allows, you can provide benefits. A call to action that creates a sense of urgency (by having an expiration date) along with contact information are critical components of a coupon.

Get Top-quality Baby Items for Less Money

Your baby deserves the best, but why pay full price for it?

Shop at Once Again Children's Consignments and:

➤ **Save Money:** Up to 90% off retail prices
➤ **Get Top Quality:** All merchandise passes a Good-As-New Test
➤ **Save Time:** Get all your baby needs in one place

Don't waste time and money!
Stop by today for the best prices and the best selection.

999 West St. | Smithville | (222) 555-9999 | Next to FoodMart

---

Get the Best for Less

10% off
any purchase
of $50.00 or more

Expires November 30, 2007
Not valid on prior purchases
Not valid on sale items

Once Again
Children's
Consignments

EXAMPLE 5

Newsletter

Once Again Children's Consignments distributes a quarterly newsletter that tells new and existing customers about the store's latest stock and requests items for the next season. The newsletter demonstrates how to use copy to promote your business. Note that a real-world newsletter would most likely include additional articles of interest to bring added value.

Adding a theme to a quarterly newsletter can be interesting for recipients. Once Again Children's Consignments might choose a holiday theme for a fourth quarter newsletter. Alternatively, a first quarter newsletter could incorporate a new beginnings and resolutions theme. For example, an audience of mothers might enjoy holiday recipes in the December newsletter or tips that would save them time and money for family gatherings. However, only use themes when they are appropriate for the business, the brand, and the target audience. If a theme will not add value for recipients, don't use it. Newsletters are also a great place to highlight customer success stories and testimonials or articles about or by experts.

In this newsletter, notice how two business-related topics were turned into promotional articles to hype new stock and acquire future stock. Review your business and objectives for the newsletter to find areas where you can inject promotional copy. Printed newsletters can be very expensive, so be sure that you will achieve your return on investment. If you have a large database of current email addresses, consider email newsletters as a less expensive option. However, you must make sure that your customers have agreed to opt in to receiving emails from your business, and they must have a way to opt out if they no longer want to receive them. Furthermore, make sure your newsletter brings some form of added value to recipients or else it may be viewed as nothing more than email in-box clutter.

Once Again News

December 2007   *Expect the best for less!*   **Volume 1 Issue 4**

Winter Merchandise Now Available

Believe it or not, the cold is coming! That means Once Again Children's Consignments has already worked hard to find the best winter clothing to offer you the widest selection at the lowest prices.

Stop by today and take a look at our full line of winter clothing, including:

Outerwear: Jackets, snowpants, mittens, gloves, scarves, hats, boots and more

Clothing: Shirts, pants, socks, dresses, skirts, shoes and more

Baby and Children's Winter Weather Gear: Car seat and stroller covers, baby slings, baby carriers and more

Toys: Sleds, snow toys, indoor toys for when it's just too cold to go outside and more

Holiday Items: Christmas and other winter holiday merchandise including decorations, clothes, accessories and more

We're sure you'll find something you need from our wide variety of winter children's items and nonseasonal merchandise.

As always, all items must pass our **Good-As-New Quality Test**, so you can feel confident you're buying only the best for your baby when you shop at Once Again Children's Consignments. Hurry in while supplies last!

Special December Holiday Hours

December 10-23: open 8:00 a.m. to 9:00 p.m.
December 24, 25 and 31: closed
All other days: open 10:00 a.m. to 6:00 p.m.

Courtesy of **Once Again Children's Consignments**

Once Again Children's Consignments
999 West St.
Smithville, XX 99999

Phone: (222) 555-9999
Fax: (222) 555-8888
Email: jdoe@onceagainchildrens.com

Owner & Editor: Jane Doe

Calling Spring Clothing Consigners

With the winter season picking up steam, it's time to start thinking about building our stock for the spring.

Before you pack up your kids' warm weather clothes, take some time to sort through them. There are undoubtedly many items that are in great condition, but for whatever reason, they're just not right for your children.

Why not make some money on these clothes instead of letting them sit in your attic or closet for another season? You can use the money you make to buy different clothes or other baby items that are just right for you and your family!

Give us a call at 222-555-9999 to discuss our consigning opportunities and start earning money now!

EXAMPLE 6
Refrigerator Magnet

A magnet is a take-away item that is created to stay in front of the customer. In this example, the refrigerator magnet provides all the information customers need so they constantly are reminded how great it is to shop at Once Again Children's Consignments. Don't waste your investment in giveaways and promotional items that don't drive sales. Instead, include a targeted message to drive sales whenever possible.

Top-quality at Low Prices

- ➤ Up to 90% off retails prices*
- ➤ Good-As-New quality tested
- ➤ Full line of baby and children's items
- ➤ Convenient location and hours

Don't waste time and money.
Shop at Once Again Children's Consignments today for all your baby's needs.

*Savings based on suggested retail price for new merchandise.

999 West. St. | Smithville | (222) 555-9999
Next to FoodMart | Open 7 days 10-6

chapter eighteen

Be Confident, and Go for It

PUTTING IT ALL TOGETHER

Whether you are writing for a small business or large company, the basic principles of creating effective copy remain the same. By following the tips in this book, you will be able to not only capture the attention of your audience but also compel them to purchase the product or service you are advertising. Remember, increased sales typically generate higher profits for your business, so invest an adequate amount of time into creating kick-ass copy that will reap the highest rewards. Keep in mind that most marketing collateral and advertisements are throw-away pieces. Your customers are not likely to keep your ad on a bookshelf with their John Grisham collection or TiVo your commercials to watch again and again. Therefore, your marketing pieces and ads should be timely, but don't agonize over them. It's OK to take risks and test copy, concepts, or ad placement if your budget allows. If you make mistakes, you'll have the opportunity to learn from them and improve with your next ad or marketing project.

For your copywriting to be successful, you must first define the goals for your ad or marketing piece. Once you have developed specific goals and ways to measure your success, you can consult your Copywriting Outline to determine which copy points will best communicate the message you need to persuade your target audience to act.

Developing the copy for your ad is a simple process. Determine the audience and media for your ad and pick and choose the appropriate copy from the information in your Copywriting Outline to develop the best message for each specific ad or marketing piece you want to produce.

Don't be afraid to test copy and take risks, but do weigh risks against rewards before you invest your marketing and advertisting dollars into each new campaign.

Professional copywriters will tell you not to reinvent the wheel each time you tackle a new project. You already have all the information you need in your Copywriting Outline to produce a compelling, professional ad. Use it, and reuse it. Marketers like to call this developing consistency around your brand and message. It's really just a matter of getting the right message to the right people at the right time. Unless your business radically changes, your message will most likely be similar from one ad to another. Just tailor that message into the best and most actionable copy possible for your target audience and medium. Once you've successfully introduced yourself to your customers and captured their attention, stay true to your message and image. Not only will your advertising and copy benefit from consistency but your brand will, too.

I LIKE WHAT THEY'RE DOING

A critical element of producing effective ads and copy is to understand what your competition is doing. Research your competitors until you know them as well as you know your own business and products. Take the time to watch and read ads and marketing materials, not only from your competitors, but from all businesses and industries. This will help you get ideas for your own ads. When you see a concept or copy point that compels you to act, write it down in your Copywriting Outline. It may be something you can use in your next advertising project. Just remember, be careful not to plagiarize your competitors or other advertisers.

THE FINE ART OF PERSUASION

Most importantly, be persuasive. Don't simply list the features and benefits of your product. Make sure your customers believe they can't live without your product or service. Make them drool for it. Capitalize on your customers' emotional triggers, and make it very obvious why *not* choosing your product or service would be a terrible mistake. Copywriting is neither a time to be modest or subtle, nor a time to assume your customers understand you or have any knowledge about your product or service. Shove your product in your customers' faces and leave no room for doubt. Don't forget to put your copy through the SLAP test, and make sure your audience knows who you are, what you do, and why you're the best. Create a perceived need and make it easy for your customers to get your product with a clear call to action. Now you're on your way to boosting sales with compelling, sales-oriented copy.

For example, an ad for a pet boarding facility could advertise, "We offer playtime for your pet." This copy simply lists the features offered by the pet boarding facility. The list of features could be more persuasive by saying, "Your dog will enjoy fun in the sun during six hours of playtime with our active, animal-loving staff." Of course, the owner could add benefits and differentiators to make it even more persuasive, but simply adding some descriptive language will help persuade a customer to call you and not your competition.

As a small business owner, you probably have some training or experience in the art of making the sale, which typically includes a strong focus

Put yourself in your customers' shoes. What would you need to know about your product or service to act?

on understanding your customer and using persuasive language. Let that knowledge and experience work to your advantage as you write your ad copy, and apply those techniques to your copywriting. Ultimately, you'll develop an additional form of brand consistency because your advertising message and communication style will mirror your sales pitch.

WHEN IN DOUBT, ASK FOR HELP

Remember, as the business owner and copywriter, you are undoubtedly biased toward your product and business. What would stop a customer from buying from you? If you find yourself having trouble detaching yourself enough to write and edit your copy with an impartial eye, don't hesitate to ask someone who doesn't work with you for their help and opinion. It might be easier for a coworker, family member, or friend to look at your ad from the customer's perspective.

Be open to criticism so you will be able to create the most effective copy. After all, you can only earn a significant return on your advertising investment if your copy compels customers to act and buy your product. For example, you might think one of your best features is a 30-day return policy; your customers, however, might not find that to be a compelling enough reason to do business with you. An impartial critic may point out to you that most of your competitors offer the same policy or your customers rarely return items. Being open to criticisms like these will help you create the best customer-oriented copy.

DESIGN COMPLEMENTS COPY

Once you have your final copy elements together, don't be afraid to create a rough layout (manually or on a computer) with section headings to ensure that your designer understands your intention for each copy element. For example, if you want to include a bulleted list in your copy, be sure to tell your designer. Also, ask your designer if he or she has any ideas for drawing attention to specific elements of your copy. Be careful not to revise your copy just because he or she wants to win a graphic design award. Remember, your designer is not a copywriter and does not know your product and audience as intimately as you do. You're the boss, and ultimately, you call the shots. While I never have a problem with designers suggesting layout nuances that may enhance my message, I would never cut or add copy strictly to fit a design. I need to have a very good reason to rewrite my copy to match a designer's layout.

Your copy is your message. While a design might capture your target audience's attention and help important points stand out, it's your copy that will drive them to action and persuade them to buy your product. Don't sacrifice your copy for a design. By placing an ad or printing a marketing piece, you're spending valuable advertising dollars. Use that money intelligently. Invest in targeted advertising and messaging with an appropriate design and customers will come.

BANKING ON RESULTS

This book is meant to teach you how to write effective copy, but I would be remiss if I didn't mention the importance of tracking the results of your marketing efforts to determine which initiatives deliver the highest return on investment. One part of your tracking strategy should include analyzing the effectiveness of your copy. If your budget allows for it, test different headlines or calls to action in different ads or marketing pieces. Then analyze the results to determine which copy tactics are generating the highest responses and meeting your specific goals for that ad or marketing piece. Use the information you gather through results tracking to improve your copywriting techniques and strategies for your future marketing initiatives.

IT REALLY IS THAT SIMPLE

Copywriting is truly easy. If you do your research and prep work, your copy will shine. Don't be afraid to take calculated risks and learn from your mistakes, but don't waste your limited advertising budget. By doing the legwork first and thoroughly completing your Copywriting Outline, you'll have a working document you can use as a tool to produce all your copywriting projects now and in the future. Spend some time up-front to develop a first-rate Copywriting Outline, and you'll reap the rewards later with a boost in sales and profits and a higher return in your advertising investments. Now kick some ass!

Layman's Glossary

WHILE IT'S EASY TO FIND VERBOSE, TECHNICAL DEFINITIONS OF MARKETING terms and phrases, it's harder to find simple, understandable explanations for the nonmarketing professional. Many small business owners and freelance writers do not have formal training or experience in marketing, so I'm including a glossary that provides layman's definitions of the marketing verbiage used throughout this book.

$10 words and $1 words: $10 words are big words that are used to make the writer sound more knowledgeable but do not add value. Simpler words (called $1 words) are thought to be generally more effective and conversational.

80/20 rule: 20% of your customers are responsible for 80% of your sales. Those 20% are your most valuable customers.

Active voice: A sentence written in the active voice shows that the subject is performing an action. For example: The cat bit Jane. Also, see *passive voice*.

Ad placement: The medium, format, and timing of when your ad will run. By purchasing ad placement with a medium, you're reserving the space and time the ad will appear. Also called *media buying*.

Bait and switch: Offering or promising something in an advertisement or marketing piece to lure customers and then changing the offer to something else at the time of purchase.

Benefit: What a product can do for the customer or how the product can help the customer.

Blog: A website that includes frequently updated entries (called posts) appearing in reverse chronological order. The term *blog* was created by combining the words *web* and *log*.

Brand: The image a person, business, product, or service portrays in the marketplace.

Business-to-business (B-to-B): Marketing and other business efforts targeted to businesses (e.g., business partners, clients, etc.).

Business-to-consumer (B-to-C): Marketing and other business efforts targeted to end-user customers.

Callout: In print ads, a callout appears in a separate, attention-getting design set apart from the main copy, so customers are certain to see it. Callouts generally include the most important messages.

Copywriting: The use of words in a marketing communication to drive an audience to action.

Corporate rhetoric: Empty, insincere, and pretentious language used to expound the virtues of an organization.

Deceptive advertising: Advertising that misleads customers by making false claims and/or omitting restrictions and necessary disclaimers. See *disclaimer*.

Demographic profile: A complete description of the various characteristics that make up your customer base. By creating a demographic profile, you can group like customers together. See *market segmentation* and *target audience*.

Differentiator: Aspects of your product, service, or business that are different than your competitors'.

Disclaimer: Used to provide details about an offer or product to protect the advertiser and ensure customers fully understand an offer. A method to provide full disclosure to a customer.

Early adopters: Those customers who are usually first to try a new product.

Elastic: An elastic product's demand is greatly affected by the price of the product. Sales will drop if the price for the product goes up, and sales will increase when the price goes down. Nonessentials are often elastic products. For example, when clothes are on sale, stores typically sell more.

Emotional trigger: A psychological, internal reaction to a stimulant. For example, the emotion of fear can be triggered by a stimulant of seeing a snake (for people who are afraid of snakes). Copywriting can appeal to customers' emotions by creating a stimulant through words that trigger those emotions.

Feature: The parts or characteristics of a product.

First person: The person speaking in a sentence (I, me, my, mine, we, us, our, ours).

Four Actions of Effective Copy: Drive, motivate, compel, persuade.

Four Rights of Advertising: The right message to the right audience at the right time and in the right place.

Inelastic: Products whose sales (i.e., the demand for the product) are not affected by price changes are considered inelastic. Most necessities are inelastic products. For example, milk sales don't typically drop if the price of milk goes up by 10%.

Jargon: Unique vocabulary belonging to a group of people that is generally not understandable to people outside of that specific group (e.g., people in a specialized industry, coworkers, etc.).

Key selling points: The features, benefits, and differentiators of a product or service that are most appropriate and actionable for a specific target audience. See *target audience*.

K.I.S.S. Rule: Keep It Simple Stupid refers to the style of copywriting in which jargon, corporate rhetoric, and complicated words are replaced with a more conversational tone and language and extraneous information is omitted.

Medium: The place where you run your ad including print (magazine, newspaper, etc.), television, radio, or online.

Opt in: Giving consumers the opportunity to agree to receive marketing communications from your organization.

Opt out: Giving consumers the opportunity to decline receiving any marketing communications from a company.

Passive voice: A sentence written in the passive voice shows that the subject is acted on, but does not perform an action. For example: Jane was bitten by the cat. Also, see *active voice*.

Perceived need: A nonessential desire for something. For example, people *need* food to live, but they don't *need* chocolate. However, advertisers can create a perceived need for chocolate with copy that convinces customers they want chocolate so badly they actually think they *need* it.

Qualitative research: Qualitative research focuses on the quality of the results gathered. For example, focus group sessions or one-on-one interviews with prospective or current customers are qualitative methods of research that allow the moderator or interviewer to have in-depth conversations with respondents. Qualitative research is usually conducted early in the process of developing a new product or marketing campaign for exploratory purposes.

Quantitative research: Quantitative research focuses on the quantity of results gathered and is used to conduct trend analysis and evaluate new business and marketing opportunities. For example, a company might conduct a survey with 1,000 current customers to determine their interest in a new product enhancement. The results will help the company develop a product enhancement that appeals to the largest number of customers, while meeting the company's financial goals. The results also help define the target audience for the new product enhancement and determine the best places to invest the advertising budget.

Red Pen Rule: Once you're done writing your copy, delete at least 30% of it to make your copy as tight and powerful as possible.

Return on investment (ROI): The amount of money that is earned as a result of an investment. For example, if it costs you $100 to design and place an ad in a local newspaper, then you want to generate enough sales from the ad to make at least $100 in profit to cover the cost of the ad. Also called *ROI*.

Second person: The person being addressed or spoken *to* in a sentence (you, your, yours).

Segment: A subgroup of a larger population within your total customer base who share similar demographic characteristics.

Seven Steps to Advertising Success: Awareness, recognition, interest, purchase, repurchase, loyalty, and influencers.

SLAP test: (**S**top, **L**ook, **A**ct, **P**urchase) The criteria your ad must meet to ensure it overtly communicates your message and obtains a desired result.

Social bookmarking: A method of saving and storing web pages in a single online location for future use or for sharing with other people.

Social media marketing: Advertising and marketing initiatives targeted to Web 2.0 such as blogs.

Social networking: Online social networking occurs through a variety of websites that allow users to interact, share content, and develop groups and communities around similar interests.

Social Web: The second generation of the World Wide Web which focuses on user-generated content, communities, networking, and interaction between users. See also *Web 2.0.*

Target audience: The group of customers that is the focus of your advertising or marketing campaign.

Third person: The person being spoken *about* in a sentence (he, his, she, her, they, them, their).

Three S's of Customer Loyalty: Stability, sustainability, and security.

T.M.I. Rule: Too Much Information refers to avoiding extraneous information in copywriting that adds no value to the overall message or for the target audience.

Web 2.0: The second generation of the World Wide Web which focuses on user-generated content, communities, networking, and interaction between users. See also *Social Web.*

Appendix A
Copywriting Outline

Product or Service Name

_____

Target Audience

_____

STEP 1: EXPLOIT YOUR PRODUCT'S BENEFITS

Questions to ask yourself as you develop Step 1 of the Copywriting Outline:

- How is my product bet; other similar products available (i.e., the competition)?

  _____

  _____

- Why is my product the best?

  _____

  _____

- How does my product make my customers' lives easier or better?

  _____

  _____

- What descriptive words help explain my product?

  _____

  _____

- What emotional triggers affect customers who consider my product?

  _____

  _____

STEP 2: EXPLOIT YOUR COMPETITION'S WEAKNESSES

Questions to ask yourself as you develop Step 2 of the Copywriting Outline:

▪ Who is my competition?

_____

_____

▪ How are my competitors' products inferior to mine?

_____

_____

▪ What are the benefits of choosing my competitor, and how can I counter those benefits?

_____

_____

▪ How can I quantify my differentiators?

_____

_____

▪ Can I obtain customer testimonials or expert opinions?

_____

_____

▪ Can I create soft differentiators?

_____

_____

▪ What are my weaknesses, and how can I turn them into positives or strengths?

_____

_____

STEP 3: KNOW YOUR AUDIENCE

Questions to ask yourself as you develop Step 3 of the Copywriting Outline:

- Who should buy my product or who is likely to want or need it (i.e., target audience/market)?

  _____

  _____

- Who will see my ad?

  _____

  _____

- Where can I best place my ad to find my audience?

  _____

  _____

- What messages will appeal most to the audience who will see my ad?

  _____

  _____

STEP 4: COMMUNICATE W.I.I.F.M. (WHAT'S IN IT FOR ME?)

Questions to ask as you develop Step 4 of the Copywriting Outline:

▪ What is the purpose of my ad?

_____

_____

▪ How can I elaborate on my product benefits and differentiators to tell customers specifically how the product will affect their lives in a positive manner?

_____

_____

▪ How can I make my copy meaningful to customers so they can personalize it?

_____

_____

STEP 5: FOCUS ON "YOU," NOT "WE"

Questions to ask yourself as you develop Step 5 of the Copywriting Outline:

- How can I word my product's benefits and differentiators so they talk *to* the customer and not *about* me?

  _____

  _____

- Have I used "you" more than "we" in my copy?

  _____

  _____

- Is my copy interactive?

  _____

  _____

- Is my tone appropriate for my audience?

  _____

  _____

STEP 6: KNOW YOUR MEDIUM

Questions to ask yourself as you develop Step 6 of the Copywriting Outline:

- Where will I be advertising?

  _____

  _____

- How can I write copy to maximize the space provided by that medium?

  _____

  _____

- How can my copy be enhanced by the design opportunities offered from that medium?

  _____

  _____

STEP 7: AVOID T.M.I. (TOO MUCH INFORMATION)

Questions to ask yourself as you develop Step 7 of the Copywriting Outline:

▪ What information is important to me but not helpful in an ad (i.e., may be useful in a news article or brochure in the future)?

_____

_____

▪ How can I keep my ad copy from becoming cluttered?

_____

_____

▪ Have I deleted filler words?

_____

_____

▪ Have I eliminated $10 words and jargon?

_____

_____

▪ Have I deleted extraneous information?

_____

_____

STEP 8: INCLUDE A CALL TO ACTION

Questions to ask yourself as you develop Step 8 of the Copywriting Outline:

▪ What is my call to action?

_____

_____

▪ What do I want my customers to do as soon as they read my ad?

_____

_____

▪ How can I create a sense of urgency?

_____

_____

▪ Is my copy written in the active voice?

_____

_____

STEP 9: C.Y.A. (COVER YOUR ASS)

Questions to ask yourself as you develop Step 9 of the Copywriting Outline:

▪ What are some phrases I need to remember to include in my ads to protect myself?

_____

_____

▪ Is there anything else I need to remember to back up my claims?

_____

_____

▪ Can I deliver on the promises and claims made in my copy?

_____

_____

▪ Can I prove my claims?

_____

_____

STEP 10: PROOFREAD

Questions to ask yourself as you develop Step 10 of the Copywriting Outline:

▪ Who can proofread my ad for me?

_____

_____

▪ What tools are available to help me proofread my ad?

_____

_____

ADDITIONAL NOTES

Use this space to make quick notes for future reference and incorporation into your Copywriting Outline.

_____

_____

_____

_____

_____

_____

_____

_____

_____

_____

_____

_____

_____

_____

_____

_____

_____

_____

_____

_____

_____

_____

_____

_____

Appendix B
Additional Copywriting and Marketing Resources

Blogs

Copyblogger.com: The most popular blog about online copywriting written by Brian Clark, an internet marketing strategist and web content developer.

Bly.com/blog: Written by one of the most successful and well-known copywriters, Bob Bly.

CopywritingMaven.com: Written by Roberta Rosenberg, a direct marketing and copywriting specialist with over 20 years of experience.

DirectCreative.com/blog/: Written by Dean Reick, a feelance copywriter with experience writing for over 200 brands.

Brandcurve.com and **MarketingBlurb.com:** Written by Susan Gunelius, freelance writer and copywriter with over a decade of experience writing copy for some of the largest companies in the world.

Websites

Bly.com: The website of one of the most well-known copywriters, Bob Bly, with links to his books, articles, and more.

Entrepreneur.com: Website dedicated to small business owners offering a variety of marketing, advertising, branding, and copywriting articles.

About.com Guide to Web Logs (http://weblogs.about.com): Through About.com (a *New York Times* Company), Susan Gunelius teaches readers about business, professional, and personal blogging.

Online Copywriting Courses

AbsoluteClasses.com: The Absolute Write University offers a variety of writing courses including Susan Gunelius' course, Copywriting in 10 Easy Steps.

AWAIonline.com: The American Writers and Artists Institute offers a variety of courses including copywriting instruction.

Books

The Copywriter's Handbook (Holt Paperbacks, April 4, 2006): Written by one of the most well-known copywriters, Bob Bly.

The Adweek Copywriting Handbook (Wiley, December 11, 2006): Written by popular copywriter, Joseph Sugarman.

Instant Advertising (McGraw-Hill, December 19, 2005): Written by Bradley J. Sugars, a professional business coach, entrepreneur, and author.

The 22 Immutable Laws of Marketing (HarperBusiness, April 27, 1994): Written by Al Ries and Jack Trout; an easy, straight-forward book about marketing.

Kellogg on Branding (Wiley, September 29, 2005): Edited by Alice Tybout and Tim Calkins; an excellent primer to branding.

Foundations of Marketing (Palgrave Macmillan, October 14, 2005): Written by Jonathon Groucutt; an excellent primer to marketing.

Ultimate Guide to Direct Marketing (Entrepreneur Press, October 4, 2005): Written by Al Lautenslager; a comprehensive resource to learn about direct marketing.

Ultimate Small Business Marketing Guide (Entrepreneur Press, January 4, 2007): Written by James Stephenson with Courtney Thurman; a complete introduction to marketing basics for small business owners.

Index